Guide To The Recommended
COUNTRY INNS
Of New England

Guests—

Ye are welcome here,
   be at your ease
Go to bed when you're ready
   get up when you please.
Happy to share with you
   such as we've got
The leak in the roof
   the soup in the pot.
Ye don't have to thank us,
   or laugh at our jokes
Sit deep and come often
   you're one of the folks.

found in an inn, Brookline Mass

SEVENTH EDITION

Guide To The Recommended

COUNTRY INNS

Of New England

Elizabeth Squier

Illustrated by Olive Metcalf

The Globe Pequot Press

Chester, Connecticut 06412

Library of Congress Catalogue Number: 73–83255
ISBN: 0–87106–961–x

Manufactured in the United States of America
Seventh Edition
Second Printing, 1981
Third Printing, 1982

First Edition, 1974
Second Edition, 1976
Third Edition, 1977
Fourth Edition, 1978
Fifth Edition, 1979
Sixth Edition, 1980

Book design by Barbara Marks

How this guide is arranged

The inns are listed by states, and alphabetically by towns within each state. The states are arranged by a peculiar whim of the publisher in the following order: Connecticut, Rhode Island, Massachusetts, Vermont, New Hampshire, and Maine. Before each state listing is a map and special index to help you in planning a trip, and on page 350 is a complete index of every inn in the book.

The abbreviations - The following abbreviations are used:

EP - European Plan—Room without meals.

EPB - European Plan—Room with breakfast.

AP - American Plan—Room with all meals.

MAP - Modified American Plan—
Room with breakfast and dinner.

BYOB - Bring Your Own Bottle.

The pointing fingers - In the write-ups you will, from time to time, find some pointing fingers ☞ ☞ ☞ ☞ ☞ While I have not rated the inns, when I found something particularly outstanding or different, I inserted a ☞ as a special note.

And the E symbol - At the end of some of the write-ups you will find this symbol:

E - Stands for Elizabeth

This was to give me the opportunity to add an individual note on a special, personal delight.

How to enjoy this guide

When I first started writing *The Guide To The Recommended Country Inns Of New England* back in 1973, I had no idea that there were so many people who were tired of the monotony of motels and thruway hotels, who were willing to exchange certain conveniences for the infinitely more warming pleasure of a good country inn.

Although I make every attempt to keep our guide up-to-date, please realize that prices and menus are subject to change, as are innkeepers. If you are planning to stay overnight, or even to have a special dinner out, I recommend that you call ahead for reservations so that you will not be disappointed. Many of the inns are quite small, and it would be a shame to travel a long distance and not get in.

By my descriptions and comments I have tried to indicate whether an inn would be appropriate for children, pets, young couples, or elderly folk. But do not forget that the very reason you are passing up a motel or a hotel is for the bit of adventure and surprise you will find sitting in a weathered farmhouse, eating country cooking, chatting with a discovered friend, and finding new delight in a very old tradition.

With prices fluctuating so wildly in today's economy I now quote you an inn's current low and high rates only. This will give you a good indication, though not exact, of the prices you can expect. Also the inns in the ski country and many along the shoreline have package rates. When you call, do inquire about them.

And do not become distressed because an inn you like may not be in this book. Please understand that our definition of a country inn is that it *must* have lodging, as well as good food, and *must* be open essentially year-round. It is all right, however, if it closes for a month or a bit more for refurbishing, or, as an instance, to avoid the uniquely New England "mud season" of late winter. With the skyrocketing cost of oil several more northerly inns have had to extend their closing periods. I have eased the rules a bit to keep these good inns in the book. If you have an inn recommendation, please write me so that I can review it for the next edition.

And a special note hopefully to dispel a rumor that has been going about. There is no charge of any kind for an inn to be in this guide.

So, enjoy! This GUIDE was compiled for you, fellow lovers of New England Country Inns.

Elizabeth

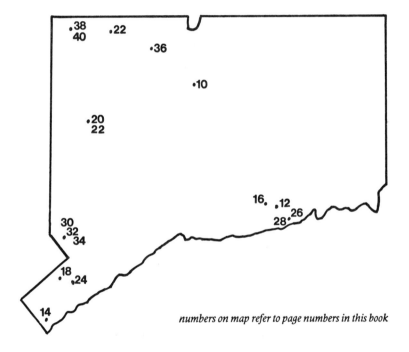

38
40
22
36
10
20
22
16
12
28 26
30
32
34
18
24
14

numbers on map refer to page numbers in this book

Connecticut

olive Metcalf

Old Farms Inn
Avon, Connecticut
06001

Innkeepers: Anne and Louis Panos
Telephone: 203-677-2818
Rooms: Five, all with private bath.
Rates: $42 EP, double occupancy.
Facilities: Open all year, restaurant closed Mondays. Lunch, dinner, Sunday champagne brunch, bar, swimming. The restaurant has wheelchair accessibility. There is also an adjacent motel.

The inn is one of the 20 oldest inns in America, established in 1757. It was here that the Boston, Hartford and Albany stage stopped overnight, and passengers and horses were accommodated.

The heart of the inn is the Coach Room, which is charmingly gracious. The Tavern Bar is panelled in barn siding. The grillroom is hung with unusual lanterns and pottery. The Forge Room and Bar, which was the original blacksmith shop, make up the rest of the inn.

The former horse stalls make comfortable nooks, and

☛ the moose head is gigantic, the largest I have ever seen. Many antique tools are on display, as are a pair of antique bicycles at the entrance to the Forge.

The ☛ "Bountiful Champagne Buffet Brunch" on Sundays has become a ritual. It consists of over 28 assorted dishes, both hot and cold, fabulous desserts, and, of course, champagne. The regular mealtimes offer you a chance to sample the wide menu. A good example is the ☛ Veal Sentino, a house specialty printed, with the inn's permission, on page 53 of Craig Claibourne's current Pierre Franey book, called *Veal Cookery*. The shellfish cocotte baked in sherry is yummy, as is the spinach salad.

The inn's location is in the middle of everything, and especially among some of the greatest shops you have ever found.

How to get there: The inn is 15 minutes west of Hartford at the intersection of Routes 44 and 10.

E: *If I lived a bit closer I would never miss that Sunday brunch.*

A well run inn and a man on a diet
go together about as well as
an arsonist and a bale of hay.

Griswold Inn
Essex, Connecticut
06426

Innkeepers: Bill and Victoria Winterer
Telephone: 203-767-0991
Rooms: 19, all with private bath, three suites.
Rates: $34 to $38, EPB, double occupancy; suites slightly higher.
Facilities: Open every day of the year except Christmas. Continental breakfast for guests, lunch, dinner, children's menu, bar.

Essex is a special place, and "The Gris" is one of the things that makes this river town so appealing. Essex, though settled long before the Revolution, is still a living, breathing, working place, not a recreated museum of a town. The first warship of the Continental Navy, the *Oliver Cromwell*, was built and commissioned here in 1776.

When you come in from the cold to the welcome of ☞ crackling fireplaces, you are doing what others have done before you for 200 years. You can lunch or dine in the cool dimness of the Library, or the Gun Room. A special spot is the Steamboat Room where the 🖛 mural on the far wall floats gently, making you feel that you are really on the river. Their collection of 🖛 Currier & Ives is museum-size and quality. 🖛 There is music almost every night, old time banjoes, sea chanteys, Dixieland jazz, or just good piano; but 🖛 never rock 'n roll.

The rooms are old, but nice. The *Oliver Cromwell* suite is in the main building, with a wood-burning fireplace, comfortable couches, a four-poster bed, and a lovely bar for your very own. There is a very nice view of Middle Cove from here.

In the bar is a great, old-fashioned popcorn machine. Bill Winterer gives popcorn to all 🖛 the children who come in, and do ask for it. It's one of many personal touches that make this nice kind of inn such a special place.

Up river in Middletown Bill has another inn, Town Farms Inn. At this time there are no rooms, but the food is divine.

How to get there: Take the Connecticut Turnpike to Exit 69, and follow Route 9 north to Exit 3. Turn left at the bottom of ramp to a traffic light, turn right and follow this street right through town to the river. The inn is on your right, about 100 yards before you get to the river.

E: *My favorite thing about The Gris? Love that popcorn machine in the bar.*

The Homestead Inn
Greenwich, Connecticut
06830

Innkeepers: Lessie Davison and Nancy Smith
Telephone: 203-869-7500
Rooms: 13, all with private bath.
Rates: $60 to $120, EPB, double occupancy.
Facilities: Closed Good Friday, Christmas, New Year's Day, and Labor Day. Continental breakfast for house guests, lunch Monday through Friday, dinner seven days a week, bar.

Jacques Thiebeult, the French chef who oversees the superb food in the inn restaurant, called La Grange, should receive many stars.

Let us start with the hors d'oeuvres, eight of them, from mushrooms marinated in a Madagascar pepper sauce, little necks baked with duxelles and herbs, to pate. Soups are scrumptious. The Billi-Bi is a hot mussel soup. If you are lucky they will have the ☞ Creme de Laiture, a velvet blend of lettuce and peas. The entrees are beef, veal, ☞ poached mousse of salmon napped with a creamy champagne sauce, plus daily specials. As for the desserts, the white chocolate mousse is the best I have ever eaten, and the gateau "Belle Haven" will make you think you are in heaven. Need I say more.

The inn's rooms are all named, and beautifully refurbished. The Poppy Room is a single with the smallest bathtub I believe was ever made. The Tassle Room has his and her desks, the Sleigh Room has old sleigh beds, and the Robin Room has delicate stencils on the wall. They were found under six layers of wallpaper dating back to 1860. The Bride's Room has a canopied queen-sized bed. All have electric blankets, TV, and clock radios.

And for a quiet drink to end a day there is no finer spot than the bar. It is called, rather nicely, The Chocolate Bar.

How to get there: Going north or south on I-95, take Exit 3. Go north about 200 yards to a light, turn left on Horseneck Road, go to the dead end, and turn left. Go under the turnpike and up a hill. The inn is on your right.

E: *The ironstone place settings in Wedgewood's Chinese Bird pattern and the beautiful stemware are for me.*

Copper Beech Inn
Ivoryton, Town of Essex, Connecticut
06442

Innkeepers: Paul and Louise Ebeltoft
Telephone: 203-767-0330
Rooms: Five, doubles with private bath.
Rates: $55 to $85, EPB, double occupancy.
Facilities: Closed Mondays, December 24 and 25, and January 1. Greenhouse cocktail lounge open all year except on Mondays and above dates. Breakfast for house guests. Lunch and dinner. Music in the Greenhouse and in the restaurant foyer on Sundays.

The magnificent copper beech tree that shades the front lawn of this wonderful inn was inspiration for the name.

The rooms are charming, with antiques, comfortable beds, and unbelievable old-fashioned bathrooms. Lots of ☛ soft towels are a real plus.

The four dining rooms all have comfortable Chippendale or Queen Anne chairs except for the dining porch that is my favorite, and it is done in white wicker. The ☛ spacious tables are spread wide apart for gracious dining. ☛ Fresh flowers are everywhere, and the waiters serving the excellent Four Star fare are friendly and efficient.

There are at least 15 or 16 appetizers to start the menu, each one better than the next. The soups that follow are superb. The lobster bisque has chunks of lobster in it, as it should. The chilled Billi-Bi is excellent. Lunch at the inn is fun and so good. Dinner by candlelight is perfection. The menu changes three or four times a year, but to give you an idea: salmon in puff pastry with sole mousse and a salmon supreme sauce, or medallions of veal, or one of my very favorites, Chateaubriand, tender tenderloin of beef surrounded by fresh vegetables.

And for dessert there are about 16 choices, all made fresh here at the inn. Do try the white chocolate mousse. I like it here as I think you can tell.

How to get there: The inn is located one mile west of Connecticut Route 9, from Exit 3 or 4. Follow the signs to Ivoryton.

E: *A turkey sandwich to go after a sumptuous dinner is my idea of a perfect Thanksgiving.*

The Roger Sherman Inn
New Canaan, Connecticut
06840

Innkeepers: Katherine Maliszewski and Steve Zur
Telephone: 203-966-4541
Rooms: 10 rooms, all with bath, all air conditioned.
Rates: $45 double occupancy.
Facilities: Closed on Sunday. Open all year. Breakfast for
   house guests only. Lunch, dinner, bar. Television in
   guest rooms, telephone, ample parking.

Built in 1740, and once the home of Roger Sherman, one of the signers of the Declaration of Independence, this friendly inn still offers a warm welcome to the tired traveler. The cuisine may be a bit more continental than it was in the early days, but we are all a bit more sophisticated today. There is music in the dining room here on the weekend.

If you are so inclined, there is a wonderful nature center just across the street from the inn, and the summer theater at Westport is still a popular place to go on a warm evening.

The guest rooms are large and comfortable. There are even two and three-room apartments, so you can bring the whole family. In the summer there is "Veranda Dining." In winter, lead me to the "Publick Tap Room."

New Canaan is a lovely little town with some very attractive shops, among them one of the very best bakeries we have ever run across. There is a good book shop, some fine dress shops, and antique shops. There is also a place called "Fat Tuesday," reputed to be the mecca for all local swingers, according to rumor only.

If you want a nice place to hole up for a week, or a month, give The Roger Sherman a try. The food is good, and the surroundings delightful.

How to get there: Take exit 37 from the Merritt Parkway and follow Route 124 north through New Canaan. One half mile beyond the town you will find the inn on your right.

*One good night in a country inn
can keep the mind in quiet order
for many moons.*

olive Metcalf

Boulders Inn
New Preston, Connecticut
06777

Innkeepers: Carolyn and Jim Woolen
Telephone: 203-868-7918
Rooms: 15, all with private bath.
Rates: $74 to $92 MAP per couple.
Facilities: Open all year. Breakfast, lunch served Memorial
  Day to Labor Day. Dinner Tuesday through Saturday
  November to Memorial Day and every day from
  Memorial Day to Labor Day. Sunday brunch Labor Day
  to Memorial Day. Bar, swimming, boating, tennis, bi-
  cycling, hiking and cross-country skiing.

The stone boulders from which the inn was made also
jut right into the inn, and so the name, Boulders Inn.
Pinnacle Mountain behind the inn offers hiking trails,
and Clea, the inn dog, will guide you up the mountain, but
beware, for she is apt to leave you to find your own way
down. From the top of Pinnacle the climber is rewarded with
a ☛ panorama that includes New York state to the west and
Massachusetts to the north.

The guest rooms all have a view either of the lake or the woods and are tastefully furnished. ☞ Eight of the rooms have fireplaces. The living room is spacious, has large windows and comfortable chairs and couches, a nice place for tea or cocktails. There is an outside terrace where, in summer, you may enjoy cocktails, dinner, and ☞ marvelous sunsets.

The food is excellent with all baking done right here. The desserts are grand. Brunch has one entree that sounds especially yummie, chicken cashew crepe. Dinner has several entrees. One favorite is Boeuf Bourguignonne, morsels of beef sauteed in cognac and baked in a rich sauce of burgundy wine, fresh mushrooms and herbs.

How to get there: From New York take I-84 to Route 7 in Danbury and follow it north to New Milford. Take a right on Route 202 to New Preston. Take 45 left and you will find the inn as you round onto the lake.

E: *Tweek is a black inn cat. Curl up in a chair with a book and Tweek will join you.*

The Inn on Lake Waramaug
New Preston, Connecticut
06777

Innkeepers: Dick & Bobbie Combs
Telephone: 203-868-2168
Rooms: 25, all with bath.
Rates: $46 per person, MAP, double occupancy; $62 to $90, MAP, single. Special weekly rates available.
Facilities: Closed Christmas, open year-round. Indoor pool (81°), game room with pool, Ping-Pong, backgammon, chess and more. Tennis, pitch-and-putt and regular golf courses, boating, swimming. Accessible to wheelchairs. Breakfast, lunch and dinner.

The second largest natural lake in Connecticut fills part of the view you have from this old colonial inn, which dates back to about 1800.

The living rooms are full of comfortable antiques, and there is a library with a fireplace for reading, or for enjoying a drink. They have ☛ an indoor, heated swimming pool with a whirlpool lagoon and sauna, plus the Barefoot Bar right at poolside. The Sandbar on the patio at the beach is open in summer, and for wintertime you have a glowing fireplace in the inn and drinks from Dudley's Tavern.

The dining rooms are spacious and well-appointed, serving good food all year-round. In summer comes an extra goodie, the Showboat Dock, and the showboat itself, which will cruise you around the 25 miles of lovely shore-line.

And for the more active there is just every kind of sport here, including free, unlimited golf at a nearby club for guests.

This is a wonderful place for the whole family.

How to get there: From New York take I-84 to Route 7 in Danbury, and follow it to New Milford. Take a right on Route 202 to New Preston. Take Route 45 left, and follow signs to the inn.

E: *The inn animals are wonderful, Zeke and Panda, and Edgar is the cat. There are also three ponies, Chester, Happy and Merry Legs.*

''The best landscape in the world
is improved by a good inn in the foreground.''
—Dr. Samuel Johnson

Silvermine Tavern
Norwalk, Connecticut
06850

Innkeeper: Francis C. Whitman, Jr.
Telephone: 203-847-4558
Rooms: 10, all with bath.
Rates: $28 to $33, single; $42 to $46, double occupancy.
Facilities: Open year-round. Closed Tuesdays from October
to May. Breakfast for house guests, luncheon, dinner,
bar. TV in parlor, six fireplaces in public rooms.

While close to everything, Silvermine Tavern still has a
way of sweeping you worlds back in time. If you wish, you
can stroll by the waterfall and feed ducks and swans on the
millpond. The colonial crossroads village known as Silvermine has been swallowed up by the surrounding towns of
Norwalk, Wilton, and New Canaan, but the Tavern still lies
at the heart of a community of great Old World beauty.

This is one of the most popular dining places in the
area, ☛ known for delicious New England traditional food.
Thursday night is set aside for a fantastic buffet supper featuring steaks, fried chicken, and many salads, all of which you

top off with a great array of desserts. Sunday buffet brunch features 20 different dishes.

Silvermine Tavern is furnished with old oriental rugs, antiques, old portraits, and great comfortable chairs and sofas surrounding huge fireplaces. The dining room overlooks the river and is decorated with over 1,000 antiques, primarily old farm tools and household artifacts.

In summer there is a ☛ brick-floored patio for al fresco dining. The guest rooms are comfortably furnished, many of them with old-fashioned tester beds.

Across the road from the Tavern you will find an authentic country store with a back room that is a museum of antique tools and gadgets. It also has a fine collection of Currier & Ives prints. Do take a leisurely drive around the back roads near the inn, too. They are a delight. Also in this area you have the well-known Silvermine Guild of Artists.

How to get there: From New York, take Exit 38 from the Merritt Parkway. Turn left onto Route 113. Turn left at the fire house onto Silvermine Avenue, which will take you directly to the inn. From I-95, take Exit 15 onto Route 7. Then take Exit 2. Turn right onto New Canaan Avenue and take your first right onto Route 123. Go by the firehouse onto Silvermine Avenue.

*I love all good inns, but secretly I have
a rather special fondness if the boniface is fat.*

Olive Metcalf

Bee and Thistle Inn
Old Lyme, Connecticut
06371

Innkeepers: Gene and Barbara Bellows
Telephone: 203-434-1667
Rooms: 10 rooms, eight with bath, two share. Double or twin beds.
Rates: $38 to $56, EP, double occupancy.
Facilities: Open all year. Breakfast, lunch, dinner, brunch on Sundays, bar. In winter dinner is served Wednesday through Monday. Closed Tuesday in winter for lunch and dinner. Dinner reservations are suggested. Private parties, bicycles for guests.

If you are looking for a country inn that is like a lovely country house, seek no further. The Bee and Thistle, set among wide lawns, beneath tall trees, provides abundance in comfort. You can have ☛ breakfast in bed, on a flower-bedecked tray. The softest supercale sheets adorn the beds. From the back of the house, you can see the Lieutenant River meandering through the meadows toward the Sound.
The menu is small, featuring fresh fish, fresh vege-

tables, homemade entrees, soups and chowder, all carefully and creatively prepared. Reservations are a must. Dinners are served by candlelight, and the dining rooms are filled with flowers. Frequently the sounds of Barbara and other musicians waft through the dining rooms. You may hear early ballads, with dulcimer and guitar, or baroque sonatas played with recorders. Plants, books, and magazines are in the lounge near the fireplace. There are six fireplaces in this old house, which was built in 1756 as a private residence.

The Old Lyme Art Association and Griswold House Historical Museum are nearby, close enough for a stroll. And there are many things to do in the area. The summer theatre at Ivoryton, the Goodspeed Opera House in East Haddam, and the charming river town of Essex are all within a short drive.

How to get there: Traveling north on Route 95, take Exit 70. At the bottom of the ramp, turn left. At traffic light turn right. At next traffic light turn left. The inn is on the right. Traveling south on route 95, take Exit 70. Turn right at the bottom of the ramp, and the inn is on the right.

E: *In just a few years the Bellows have made some grand changes in this lovely old inn.*

Old Lyme Inn
Old Lyme, Connecticut
06371

Innkeepers: Kenneth and Diana Milne
Telephone: 203-434-2600
Rooms: Five, all with bath.
Rates: $35 to $40, continental breakfast included.
Facilities: Open all year. Closed on Mondays. Continental breakfast, lunch, dinner.

The food here is 🐄 excellent and unusual. From the fresh soup stocks to the 🐄 pastry shells, everything is homemade, as are all of the desserts, so tender and flakey. The menu changes delightfully every three or four months. Some entrees I have tried and thoroughly enjoyed are Filet Mignon, with a green peppercorn sauce, Quinelle of halibut, and chicken served in cider with apples. They usually have a special of the day, and whatever it is, try it. You may gain a little weight, but you will enjoy yourself immensely.

Throughout the inn the chairs are blue velvet, luxuriously soft and comfortable. The large cocktail lounge has a bar that seats six, and a 🐄 back bar the innkeepers found in

Philadelphia that is over 100 years old. This back bar has a bevelled mirror that most museums would covet.

In addition to the two-level, lovely main dining room, there is a private room off the lobby for eight to 12 people, a real nice way to entertain good friends.

There is much to do in this area, with antique shops all over, the beautiful Connecticut River two minutes away, historic Essex just across the river, and a small, interesting museum called The Florence Griswold House almost directly across the street. Here you will get a fascinating glimpse of the art colony that flourished in Old Lyme at the beginning of the century.

How to get there: Traveling north on I-95 take Exit 70 immediately on the west side of the bridge. At the bottom of ramp turn left. Take the first right at the traffic light, and turn left at the next light. The inn is on the right. Traveling south on I-95, take Exit 70. At the bottom of the ramp turn right. The inn is on the right.

E: *The bar is a real favorite spot of mine, with a bartender who remembers what you drink.*

Where else, in all good conscience,
could I stay but at a country inn.

The Elms
Ridgefield, Connecticut
06877

Innkeepers: Robert and Violet Scala
Telephone: 203-438-2541
Rooms: Eight with private bath, one suite.
Rates: $40 per room, $45 double occupancy, $55 for the
　　　suite.
Facilities: Closed Christmas day and Wednesdays. Breakfast
　　　for house guests only. Lunch, dinner, bar, Sunday
　　　brunch. Friday and Saturday a piano.

In 1760 a master cabinetmaker built this charming
colonial house that is now known as The Elms. It is on a
historical site, for it was here that the Battle of Ridgefield was
fought during the Revolution. Since 1799, when it became
an inn, the same loving care and artistry that marked its
beginning has been applied to every phase of the operation.

There is a ☛ comfortable four-poster in one of the
quiet rooms upstairs. Another bedroom has maple spool
twin beds, and no matter which room you choose you will
have your ☛ own fireplace. The quiet charm here induces

slumber and assures the weary traveler of a restful night.

The brochure says, "To partake of a meal is no mundane experience in eating, but rather an adventure in dining." And so it is, with quail fresh from the fields, escargots flown fresh from France, and on and on, all of it delicious. The list of hors d'oeuvres is very impressive, with herring in cream, scampi romani, and smoked salmon but a few of the selections. There are five delicious soups, with the onion au gratin a special. Entrees like broiled English lamb chops with kidney and bacon, curry of sliced capon with wild rice and chutney, veal, steak, and rack of lamb, are all on the menu. The dessert list is as large as the hors d'oeuvres list, with pears burgundy, tortonis, spumoni, and an old favorite of mine, Zabaglione.

Ridgefield is a lovely town off the major highways. There are concerts in the park, tons of good shops to wander into, and good summer theater nearby.

How to get there: The inn is located at 500 Main Street in Ridgefield. Going north or south on Route 7, take Route 35 right into town.

E: *Any place that serves* *Coupe Elizabeth has to get my nod. It is bing cherries bathed in cherry herring, sprinkled with cinnamon, and poured over vanilla ice cream. Yum. Yum.*

olive Metcalf

Stonehenge
Ridgefield, Connecticut
06877

Innkeepers: David Davis and Douglas Seville
Telephone: 203-438-6511
Rooms: Eight, all with private bath and television.
Rates: $45 to $55 per room.
Facilities: Closed New Year's Day and Tuesdays. Open year-round. Breakfast, lunch, dinner, bar. Parking. Superb food and service.

"You can't go home again," said Thomas Wolfe, but you can go back to Stonehenge. Under the direction of two gentlemen, David Davis and Douglas Seville, this beautiful country inn is blooming again. The chef, ☛ Jean-Maurice Calmels, is French-born and trained, and nonpareil. The setting is still serenely beautiful, with the old white farmhouse overlooking the pond, which is bedecked with swans and aflutter with Canadian geese and ducks stopping in on their migratory journeys. The service, under the skilled direction of Maitre d'Hotel Willie, is what we always dreamed it should be; deft, quiet, pleasant, knowledgeable.

For a quiet dinner a deux, reserve a table in the bar. Address yourself seriously to the food. The appetizers are unusual, not to be skipped over lightly. The soups are poetic. The trout is live. "How long ago?" I asked. "About five minutes," was the reply. "The time it takes to come from the 'trout house.' " If you are tired of the "same old thing," book yourself into Stonehenge for a long weekend and find out what "haute cuisine" is all about. It is expensive, but worth every centime.

Many of the dishes we love so much are still served at Stonehenge. The inventive touch with vegetables, the care taken with the sauces, all reflect the dedication with which M. Calmels approaches his task.

The porch facing the pond has been enclosed, and is now the Stonehenge Room, a room with a great view.

In the re-done bar Len Gendal plays wonderful piano. He is excellent.

How to get there: Take Route 7 to Ridgefield. The inn's sign, coming south from Route 84, is not very large, but on the right.

E: *My favorite room is the big one in the front of the main house. Any season, any weather, it is a home away for us with wine and cheese waiting and continental breakfast served on the spot.*

olive Metcalf

West Lane Inn
and
The Inn at Ridgefield
Ridgefield, Connecticut
06877

Innkeepers: Maureen Mayer and Henry Prieger
Telephone: West Lane 203-438-7323,
        Ridgefield 203-438-8282
Rooms: 14, all with private bath.
Rates: $60 to $75, EPB.
Facilities: Open all year. TV, air conditioning, fireplaces. The restaurant across the driveway is closed Mondays and Tuesdays. Lunch and dinner, Sunday brunch, bar, lounge, piano nightly.

Ridgefield is a lovely town, and we have a first here, two totally separate inns next door to each other. West Lane has the rooms, and The Inn at Ridgefield has the food.

West Lane's rooms are lovely, with either queen or king-sized beds, deluxe blankets, and ☞ huge, thirsty towels. There are comfortable chairs, and the decor is magnificent. The bedrooms are really spacious, and there is ☞ a carved wood screen on the second floor you must not miss. West Lane does have a small dining room for continental breakfasts, and when you are ready for lunch or dinner you go across the driveway to The Inn at Ridgefield.

Chef Raymond Peron has a rather prestigious background, having been executive chef of the Hay-Adams Hotel in Washington, D.C., and of the S.S. *France*. He cooks superbly. There are seven or eight hors d'oeuvres, among them cold mussels in mustard sauce. A cold and a hot soup are served, and the entrees make my mouth water as I write. The duck à l'orange is a favorite, as is the Dover Sole. The inn special is a seafood platter served deliciously cold. Desserts, as expected, are grand, and a final touch are the special coffees.

Both inns are just around the corner from the famous Cannon Ball House, which was struck by a British fieldpiece during the Revolution. There are several museums in town, in addition to fine shops. You are also close to three summer theaters, Candlewood, Darien, and Westport.

How to get there: Coming north from New York on Route 684, or Route 7 from the Merritt Parkway, get off on Route 35 and follow it to Ridgefield. The inns are on Route 35 at the south end of town.

➩

E: *The ends of* *old, wooden wine and whiskey crates that line the porch of The Inn at Ridgefield let you know there are good things inside.*

Old Riverton Inn
Riverton, Connecticut
06065

Innkeepers: Pauline and Mark Telford
Telephone: 203-379-8678
Rooms: 10, all with private bath.
Rates: $35 to $37 EPB, double occupancy.
Facilities: Closed Christmas day and Mondays. Open year-round. Breakfast for house guests, lunch, dinner, bar. Dining room has wheelchair accessibility. Country store.

The village of Riverton was once called "Hitchcocksville," named after the famous Hitchcock Chairs which are still being manufactured in the old factory on the banks of the Farmington River, opposite the inn. The factory is open every day except Sunday until 5 p.m., and guests are always welcome.

Old Riverton Inn was originally opened in 1796. It was on the post road between Hartford and Albany and known as Ives Tavern. The inn was restored in 1937, and again in 1954. The  Grindstone Terrace was enclosed to make it available for year-round use. The floor of this room is made of grindstones which, according to 100-year-old records, were quarried in Nova Scotia, sent by ship to Long Island Sound, and then up the Connecticut River to Hartford. From there they were hauled by oxen to Collinsville, where they were used in the making of axes and machetes.

The colonial dining room has low ceilings, Hitchcock chairs, excellent food and ☛ home-baked breads and pastries. The Hobby Horse Bar has saddles for seats, and in charge of this charming room is a ☛ Philippine bartender who, like most of the help, has been here for years.

☛ Mints on your pillows at night is a very special touch I love. All of the rooms are cheerful, comfortable, and assure you of a good night's sleep. There is a lovely library area on the second floor that is a nice spot to relax in after looking at all of the things this charming village has to offer.

Antiques, galleries, a general store, the Hitchcock Museum, the Seth Thomas factory outlet, the Tartan Shop, Kitchen Shop, not to mention the Cat Nip Mouse Tearoom, are all here.

How to get there: Take Route 8 or Route 44 to Winsted. Turn east on Route 20, and it is 3½ miles, just over the river, to the inn.

E: *The drive between the inn and East Hartland or Granby on Route 20 is one of the most scenic in this state.*

Under Mountain Inn
Salisbury, Connecticut
06068

Innkeepers: Lorraine and Albert Bard
Telephone: 203-435-0242
Rooms: Seven, each with bath.
Rates: $52 to $59 double occupancy, EPB.
Facilities: The inn is closed in March. Also on Monday and
    Tuesday. Breakfast for house guests, brunch on Satur-
    day and Sunday, 11:30 to 2:30. Dinner Wednesday
    through Saturday, 5 to 10 p.m. On Sunday, 1:30 to 7 p.m.

What joy to find an old inn that had closed up reopened
under new ownership. The Bards looked long and hard at
many country inns before they found Under Mountain.
They have come east from California, and the West Coast's
loss is certainly our gain. Under Mountain, in case you didn't
know, is really an old colonial house. ☞ The bar was constructed from wide, old boards hidden in the attic. Boards as
wide as these were made from trees known before the revolution as "king's wood," which was reserved for the special
use of His Majesty. They certainly make a lovely bar.

The rooms are very well done, with antiques, comfortable beds, and ☞ bathrooms that are really knockouts. There is a library on the second floor so you can read away to your heart's content.

Though the house is old and colonial and full of years, the food is slightly sophisticated with such delightful things as Escargots in Mushroom Caps, Steak au Poivre, poached salmon, and even sweetbreads. The soups and breads are homemade, absolutely delightful, and if you have room at the end, try an apple pancake. It is wonderful to have a place open for brunch on Saturday as well as Sunday. Come really early because the ☞ Clam Pie and Kippered Herring have a tendency to be all gone, they are so popular.

How to get there: Take Route 41 north 4½ miles from Salisbury. The inn is on the left.

🔔

E: *You know me and animals. Well the inn cat is Pumpkin, and the dog is Sal.*

"Enough," he cried
and left with all speed
for the neighborhood inn.

White Hart Inn
Salisbury, Connecticut
06068

Innkeeper: John Harney
Telephone: 203-435-2511
Rooms: 17, all with private bath and air conditioning.
Rates: $22 to $40 EP, single; $24.50 to $48 EP, double.
Facilities: Open all year. Breakfast, lunch, dinner, colonial taproom.

On the village green in Salisbury sits a classic, white clapboard country inn with spacious porches, shaded by several of our few surviving, lovely wineglass elms. Inside you will find a fine blend of American and ☛ oriental cuisine.

Sweet and sour pork with lychees is a popular Mandarin dish. Tangy orange-flavored chicken balls is Szechuan. ☛ Hot, spicy leg of lamb is a Hunan favorite, and also a favorite of mine, the hotter the better. But all hot dishes served here can be ordered without the "hot." For the traditionalist there are steaks, ribs, lamb and fish, also breast of chicken with Mandarin orange sauce, all of which makes the White Hart a very interesting place to dine.

The inn has a special interest in Sarum teas. They are really superior to what the average person considers tea because they come from areas of the world where fine teas are grown but not generally exported. Sarum teas are served here and also sold here.

The taproom is a nice place for travelers to gather, and you will want to visit and browse in the Country Store, just off the lobby. There you will find good home-baked goods, health foods, candies, teas and coffees. At Christmastime there is a lady, ☛ Olive Dubois, who makes a whole gingerbread village, a new one every year. It is on a table about five feet wide and 12 feet long. All of the buildings have people in them, and there are people and bands and parades all over. There is even a ski slope with skiers coming down. ☛ This village is absolutely incredible.

How to get there: The inn is at the intersection of Routes 44 and 41 in Salisbury. You get to Salisbury by going north on Route 7 from the Merritt Parkway.

E: *While I love all of Connecticut, this corner holds a special spot in my heart. Just lovely.*

Man's cruelty to man knows almost no horizons.
His continued existence, however, is justified
when he says to a stranger, ''Come in.''

numbers on map refer to page numbers in this book

Rhode Island

Olive Metcalf

The Inn at Castle Hill
Newport, Rhode Island
02840

Innkeeper: Paul McEnroe; Paul Goldblatt, general manager
Telephone: 401-849-3800
Rooms: 18, 14 with private bath.
Rates: $40 to $95, EPB, double occupancy.
Facilities: Open year-round. Breakfast, lunch and dinner in season. Bed and breakfast in January, February, and March. In other winter months dinner is served Thursday, Friday, Saturday, and Sunday. Special Sunday brunch, 12 to 5 p.m., Easter through December. Live jazz on Sunday afternoons. As for things to do, there is everything. Newport is the home of America's Cup Races, the Tennis Hall of Fame, and is famous for its great "cottages" lining the waterfront.

The Inn at Castle Hill was built as a private home in 1874. It has, over the years, undergone few changes, and the warm atmosphere has been maintained. Thirty-two acres of shoreline right on the entrance of Narragansett Bay offer a natural setting for almost anything a person could desire.

The views from anyplace, in or about the inn, are breathtakingly beautiful. ☞ The Atlantic Ocean and the bay are at your feet.

The inn has four dining rooms, and special is the small one with only six tables, each set with different serving plates. Another is a light and airy oval room, and all look over the water. ☞ All of the food is prepared to order by a fine chef. Veal, beef, roasts, lamb, fowl and seafood are prepared many ways and are beautifully served. Every day there are three homemade soups, together with an endless variety of appetizers.

The Tavern is a different room, with a beauty of a bar and a view unmatched, if you love the sea. There are Chinese teak and marble tables in the living areas, and the bannister on the staircase is its own delight.

The rooms are almost all quite large and beautifully furnished. The paneling is magnificent, as are the oriental rugs that have been left here.

Innkeeper McEnroe has refurbished the entire inn with wallpapers that are color-coordinated with spreads and drapes, plus thick towels. Here the view outside is not enough for our innkeeper. He cares about the interior look, too.

How to get there: From the north take Route 138 into Newport, then follow Thames Street to Ocean Drive. Go to the end and look for the sign on your right. From the east come across the Newport Bridge and exit onto Thames Street.

E: *The 10-mile ocean drive is among the most strikingly beautiful areas in New England.*

Olive Metcalf

Larchwood Inn
Wakefield, Rhode Island
02879

Innkeeper: Francis J. Browning
Telephone: 401-783-5454
Rooms: 11 double, seven with private bath.
Rates: $20 single, to $40 double occupancy.
Facilities: Open year-round. Restaurant, bar, formal gardens, Breachway Room for weddings, the Buttery for small private parties.

Over the fireplace in the homey bar is carved "Fast by an Ingle Bleezing Finely," a quotation from the Scots' Robert Burns. ☞ His birthday, January 25th, is celebrated here, and last year a couple of pipers came over from Connecticut to help the party along. The Scotch flavor is all over this homelike country inn. The present innkeeper, Francis J. Browning, took over from his in-laws, the Camerons, who had been running things for the past quarter of a century. The Tam O'Shanter Cocktail Lounge serves up a delectable lunch each day except Sunday, and there are four other lovely rooms for dining or private entertaining.

Come summer there is a patio in the garden, where meals are served. The inn is situated in the heart of Rhode Island's beautiful South County. Saltwater beaches for bathing, fishing, and sunning are close by. In the winter it is only a short drive to Pine Top and Yawgoo Valley for skiing.

Rhode Island isn't all that big, you know, so it's never very far from anywhere to the Larchwood Inn.

How to get there: Follow Route 1A to Wakefield, Rhode Island.

When you have but one night to spend
which inn to choose is as difficult
as the choice you had years ago
at the penny candy counter,
and equally rewarding.

Olive Metcalf

Shelter Harbor Inn
Westerly, Rhode Island
02891

Innkeepers: Jim and Debbie Dey
Telephone: 401-322-8883
Rooms: 18, 12 with baths, one with fireplace.
Rates: $35 to $55 double occupancy.
Facilities: Open every day. Breakfast, lunch and dinner. Sunday brunch. Bar. Swimming, sailing. Summer theaters nearby. Two paddle tennis courts with night lighting.

If you like a three-mile stretch of uncluttered beach located just behind a lovely, old country inn, find your way to Rhode Island and the Shelter Harbor Inn. Bring the children. There is a salt pond, too, often inhabited by one of the inn dogs, Heidi, a friendly Newfoundland. Borrow the Sunfish and spend a delightful hour or two on the water.

Eight of the guest rooms are in the restored farmhouse, and then 10 more are located in the barn. There is a large central living room here which opens onto a spacious deck, ideal for families traveling. Or if your business group is small, have a meeting right here.

The menu reflects the location of the inn, and at least half the items offered are from the sea. ☞ The Finnan Haddie is especially smoked in Narragansett. You can choose your place to eat, from the formal dining room to the more relaxed library. The sun porch has been turned into a pub bar. There is a delightful old wood stove to warm you, and Debbie's plants are everywhere. If weather permits, get to drinking on the secluded terrace.

If you can tear yourself from the beach, there is much to see around here. You are about halfway between Mystic and Newport. The ferry to Block Island leaves from Port Judith, takes an hour to cover the 12 miles, and when you arrive you will find it a super spot for bicycling. You can charter boats for fishing, or stand on the edge of the surf and cast your line into the sea. In the evenings there is Theater by the Sea in nearby Mantanuck, or the Heritage Playhouse in Hopkinton.

How to get there: Take Route 1 out of Westerly for about five miles. The inn is on the right side of the road, heading northeast.

E: *Authentic Johnny Cakes are served here. Delicious!*

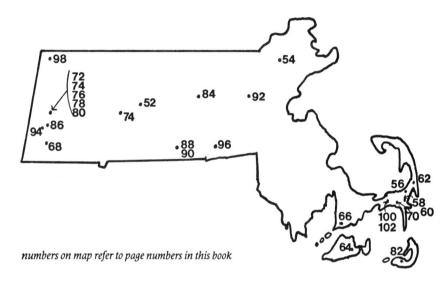

•98

72
74
76
78
80

•54

•84

•92

•52

•74

94• •86

•68

•88
90

•96

56 •62

•58 60
66 70

100
102

64

82

numbers on map refer to page numbers in this book

Massachusetts

Olive Metcalf

The Lord Jeffrey
Amherst, Massachusetts
01002

Innkeeper: David Nichols, general manager
Telephone: 413-253-2576
Rooms: 54, with private bath.
Rates: $23 to $48, EP.
Facilities: Open seven days a week since 1926. Breakfast, lunch, dinner, Sunday brunch. Tavern, dining rooms, TV in every room.

Sitting on the magnificent green in this lovely old college town is the Lord Jeffrey Inn. Lord Jeffrey Amherst, as he is known in song, was a soldier of the king, and for his brave deeds this town was named for him. The inn was, too. Although the inn was built in the twenties, it looks as if it has been here for centuries.

A very nice feature of the inn is ☞ outdoor summer dining in a delightful garden. Winter, in turn, brings bright fires in the fieldstone fireplaces and a folk singer to raise spirits in the bar.

The town of Amherst is a pretty busy place, for there are

many colleges here and nearby. It was also the home of three celebrated poets: Emily Dickinson, Eugene Field, and Robert Frost. Another renowned resident was Noah Webster. You can spend days, indeed weeks, seeing all the history that abounds..

The inn has a lovely library room that you can reserve for a private party. While all the food is good, I found that the Eggs Benedict, served for lunch, no less, were among the best I have eaten anywhere. And you will love the colonial dining room, which is extremely comfortable, spacious, and just nice to look at. The gardens are lovely, with wisteria vines that in spring are spectacular.

How to get there: From I-91, take Route 9 to Amherst. The inn is located on the Green, in the middle of town.

E: *Any inn that serves Eggs Benedict for lunch is high on my list, and when served in the beautiful dining room at The Lord Jeff, I am doubly happy.*

How good of you to have asked me in.

53

olive Metcalf

Andover Inn
Andover, Massachusetts
01810

Innkeepers: Henry Broekhoff and John Oudheusden
Telephone: 617-475-5903
Rooms: 33, 23 with private bath.
Rates: $40 EP single; to $43, EP, double occupancy.
Facilities: Open all year. Dining room is closed only on Christmas. Breakfast, lunch, dinner, bar. TV, air conditioning. Accessible to wheelchairs. Phones in every room, elevator, barber shop. Sunday brunch is special.

The inn is on the campus of Phillips Academy. You expect ivy-covered buildings, and you get them in abundance. When you walk through the gracious front door of the inn you are greeted by a wonderful living room with fireplace.

The bar in the right corner of the main entrance room is one of the coziest we have seen. ☞ The stools are over-stuffed, and so comfortable you hate to leave.

Rooms here have every modern convenience, including color TV, radio, direct dial telephone, air conditioning, and full baths, all with either a view of the delightful inn gardens, the neighboring pond, or Phillips Academy.

The dining room is elegant, with crisp napery and crystal chandeliers. The chef, one of the owners, has a Dutch background, so the food is superb. Full breakfasts and ample lunches fit well with the broad dinner menus. And there is a special Sunday brunch from 11 to 2:45 p.m. On Sundays they have a special called Rijsttafel. It is an original Indonesian dish prepared the right way, and eaten in the proper manner. It consists of dry, steamed rice and an indefinite number of side dishes and sauces. The menu tells you how to eat this fabulous feast. It is served Sunday only, from 4 to 8:45 p.m., and is by reservation.

How to get there: The inn is 25 miles north of Boston on Route 28, near the intersection of Routes 93 and 495.

✗

E: ☞ *Monday through Saturday evenings guests enjoy light classical music on the grand piano.*

*Modern man has done wonderous things
in preserving the whooping cranes
and country inns.*

Inn of the Golden Ox
Brewster, Massachusetts
02631

Innkeepers: Charles and Ruth Evans
Telephone: 617-896-3111
Rooms: Six, all share bathroom facilities.
Rates: $20 to $25, per room.
Facilities: Open all year. During off season, meals are served
    Friday, Saturday, and Sunday. TV in lounge. Parking.

Housed in an 1828 building that was once a church, the
Inn of the Golden Ox is run by a man who used to be an
Episcopal minister, until he lost his voice. It is coming back,
and when you meet Charles Evans, half German, a quarter
Swiss and a quarter Welsh, you feel that somehow, the right
thing has happened. A giant of a man, Mr. Evans welcomes
you to his inn.

The inn is small, and charmingly decorated with red-
and-white, checked tablecloths in one dining area, and
something more formal in the other. ☞ The menu, written
on blackboards, is German. Not all wurst and kraut, but truly
beautiful German cooking. Good German beer is available, as

well as a nice selection of wine and cocktails.

The rooms for travelers are small, furnished with massive Victorian pieces, much like rooms in a small European inn.

How to get there: Take Route 6A on the north side of Cape Cod to Brewster. The inn is at the intersection of 6A and Tubman Road.

E: *Do not overlook the real innkeepers, Tylos, a black labrador and Bonnie, a cocker spaniel.*

The good morning greeting and the
good night good wish can only be found in a country inn.

The Queen Ann Inn
Chatham, Massachusetts
02633

Innkeepers: Guenther and Nicole Weinkopf
  Siegfried and Traudl Kiesewetter
Telephone: 617-945-0394
Rooms: 30, all with private bath.
Rates: Single $42 to $52 EPB; double $24 to $31 per person;
  suites $38 to $50 per person EPB.
Facilities: Closed November 1 to April 15. In summer, full
  breakfast. Off season continental breakfast. Buffet
  lunch and full dinner. Sunday brunch, bar, telephones
  in every room. Tuesday clambakes.

The window at the far end of the dining room has
etched in it an old, 1680, Dutch map of New England, ☛ an
outstanding piece of work.

Queen Ann's beautifully restored public rooms include
a gracious lobby with ☛ Victorian love seats and sofas done
in soft gray velvet complimented by warm salmon and burgundy tones. The Samuel de Champlain Lounge, named
after the famous explorer whose vessel landed in Chatham

in 1606, has comfortable velvet-covered chairs and couches, the perfect atmosphere in which to relax and enjoy good friends.

The Earl of Chatham Dining Room serves delicious native seafood along with more than excellent continental cuisine. ☛ The innkeepers are international hotel people, and the menu reflects their expertise, with Viennese Tafelspitz, a sliced boiled beef rump served with chive sauce and an apple-horseradish cream; and Paela Zingara, which is saffron rice prepared with mussels, shrimp, fish, tomatoes, green peppers, all slightly seasoned with garlic. These are just a sample. The menu in its entirety is superb. If you are lucky enough to be here on a Sunday, the ☛ brunch is truly quite different.

Rooms are also excellent. Beds are either twin or king-sized. All the rooms are different and have beautiful antiques, modern bathrooms, and telephones.

There is much to do and see in the area. Sightseeing alone is a plus, with a lighthouse that has a magnificent view of the ocean, beaches for swimming, in addition to sailing, fishing, and boats for charter.

How to get there: From Route 6 take Exit 11, go south on Route 137 to its end, take a left on Route 28 to Chatham Center. At your first traffic light, in about three miles, go right on Queen Ann Road. The inn is on your right.

E: *Imagine receiving this lovely place for a wedding gift. True. It happened in 1840.*

The Town House Inn
Chatham, Massachusetts
02633

Innkeepers: Russell and Svea Peterson
Telephone: 617-945-2180
Rooms: 16 with private bath.
Rates: $55 to $65 double occupancy, EPB.
Facilities: Open all year. Breakfast only. Color, cable TV. Fireplaces in the cottages, sauna, waterbeds, and refrigeration in each room.

The front porch that overlooks Main Street beckons me. The 4th of July parade, one of the summer's biggest events, goes right by the front door. Best seat in town is the porch of this inn.

The original structure dates back to the 1820s. Remains of the foundation can still be seen in the cellar, and some of the original woodwork is still here. The carved mouldings and wood trim depict harpoon and oar motifs. The floors are made of hemlock, and the original walls, recently exposed, have hand-painted scrolling.

The 🖝 rooms are immaculate; matter of fact, the

whole inn is. If you have always wanted to try a water bed, here is your chance. I think they are neat. The rest of the beds are very comfortable, also. All of the linens and towels are laundered right here by Svea. She likes to hang them out, when weather permits, for that ☞ lovely smell of fresh air.

Breakfast is the only meal served here, but it is special. Svea makes some delicious ☞ Scandanavian goodies. Restaurants, shops, churches, beaches, golf course, tennis courts, and the library are all within walking distance of the inn.

There are three small Peterson children that help run the inn.

How to get there: Take Route 6 (mid-Cape highway) to Exit 11, Route 137 south to Route 29 and east to the center of downtown Chatham. Watch for the Eldredge library on your left. The inn is next door.

⚓

E: *The Friday night band concerts are fun.*

Nauset House Inn
East Orleans, Massachusetts
02643

Innkeepers: Lucille and Jack Schwarz
Telephone: 617-255-2195
Rooms: 14, eight baths.
Rates: $20, single; $35 to $40, double, per room.
Facilities: Open April 1 to November 1. Breakfast only, many
 great restaurants nearby. Beaches, fishing, BYOB bar.

Nauset Beach at Orleans is the first of the great Atlantic
beaches that rim Cape Cod; rolling dunes, dashing surf and
wide swaths of sand run southward for more than 10 miles.
There are quiet out-of-the-way coves that offer the beach
goer an ideal place to sun and picnic, or just to relax and
enjoy. If your tastes are for fresh water there are dozens of
inland ponds at hand.

The inn serves breakfast only, but it is an old-fashioned
country feast served by an open hearth with a floor of brick
and great family-sized tables. ☞ The patio off this room is
Cape-comfortable with wide wicker chairs, flowers, and a
pair of fierce cement dogs for guards. The view from here on

a summer day is one of real restful beauty, with the sea, a cat or two, and flowers. What more could anyone want.

The inn has its own antique shop in the rear. The parlor is filled with unusual clocks. One is a French pendicular clock of most unusual design. This room boasts a fireplace, books, game and card tables. Jack's Bar, a small one, is the spot for BYOB cocktails or morning Bloody Marys.

An old 1908 conservatory found in Greenwich, Connecticut has been reassembled and is now part of the inn. Inside is white wicker furniture, a patterned brick floor, a controlled jungle of plants, and a dolphin fountain.

☛ Jack is a great host, especially when accompanied by the inn dog, a boxer named "Ug."

How to get there: From the Mid-Cape Highway (Route 6) go to Main Street in Orleans, turn right to Beach Road, and the inn is on your right.

☾

E: *I wish I were on the patio right now with a warm sea breeze on my neck and a right Bloody Mary in hand.*

*The chill of a wood-stove-warmed bedroom
evaporates in the crisp smell of bacon for breakfast.*

The Charlotte Inn
Edgartown, Massachusetts
on Martha's Vineyard
02539

Innkeeper: Gerry Conover
Telephone: 617-627-4751
Rooms: 15 with private bath, two cottage rooms.
Rates: $58 to $90, double occupancy; off season, $28 to $78.
Facilities: Open all year. Continental breakfast, lunch in summer only. From Christmas through April, dinner on Thursday, Friday, Saturday, and Sunday, but do call for reservations. Gift Shop, sailing, swimming, fishing, golf, tennis, art gallery.

The start of your vacation is a 45-minute ferry ride to Martha's Vineyard. It's wise to make early reservations for your automobile on the ferry. There are also cabs if you prefer not to take your car.

When you open the door to the inn you are in the ☞ Edgartown Art Gallery, with interesting artifacts and paintings both water color and oil. This is a well appointed gallery featuring such artists as Ray Ellis who has a fine talent in both media. The inn also has an unusual gift shop.

Food here is French. The restaurant, called Chez Pierre, is small and intimate with excellent food. A marvelous green peppercorn sauce comes with two prime loin lamb chops. The veal, properly tender, is superb. Spinach salad that you will not forget and salmon poached in fume served with a dill sauce are winners. The desserts, needless to say, are different and oh so good.

The rooms are authentic. There are early American four-poster beds, and one suite has a ☛ queen-sized four-poster bed, plus a fireplace. All have comfortable couches and chairs, and lots of ☛ down pillows, ☛ down comforters and quilts; necessities after a walk to see the shops, sand, water or whatever you desire.

There is sailing, swimming, fishing, golf, tennis, shells, sun, shopping and theater to keep you busy.

How to get there: Reservations are a must if you take your car on the ferry from Woods Hole, Massachusetts. Forty-five minutes later you are in Vineyard Haven. After a 15-minute ride, you are in Edgartown, and on Summer Street is the inn.

♧

E: The ☛ *waiters are friendly and well informed and that makes life a bit easier and pleasanter.*

Coonamessett Inn
Falmouth, Massachusetts
02541

Innkeeper: Mrs. Gregory
Telephone: 617-548-2300
Rooms: Three double rooms, plus cottages. Baths to share.
Rates: $22 to $65 per room.
Facilities: Open seven days a week, all year. Breakfast, lunch,
  dinner, bar. Parking.

In 1796, in a rolling field that sloped gently down to a
lovely pond, Mr. Thomas Jones constructed a house and
barn that was to become Coonamessett Inn (Indian, for "the
place of the large fish.") The framework of the house is
finished with wooden peg joints, and much of the interior
paneling is original. Many of the bricks in the old fireplaces
are thought to be made of ballast brought from Europe in the
holds of sailing ships.

Don't despair if you can't get a room in the inn itself.
☛ The cottages are fine, and especially good if you are
traveling en masse, with the family. The grounds are beautiful, kept in mint condition year-round. We love the Cape off

season, and it is good to know that no matter what day we decide to come, we will receive a cordial welcome here.

The food is excellent, offered from a large, varied menu, and served by friendly waitresses. Breakfasts are memorable. Lunch attracts a large group, for this place is really well-known. And dinner is great, with lobster served four different ways. You can even have lobster sauce on your scrod. Meat eaters are not forgotten either; two favorites are featured, sweetbreads and bacon with sauce supreme, and a lamb chop mixed grill. ☛ Desserts have a menu all their own. Fantastic.

There are little shops to lure you, and all around you will see the loveliest array of grass, trees, flowers, shrubs . . . and peace. Don't forget the peace.

How to get there: Take Route 28 at the bridge over the canal, and go into Falmouth. Turn left on Jones Road, and at the intersection of Gifford Street you will see the inn.

E: *I wish I lived closer, because I like the whole thing, starting with the flower arrangements, fresh every other day, that are done by a man who really knows how to arrange.*

olive Metcalf

Windflower Inn
Great Barrington, Massachusetts
01230

Innkeepers: Barbara and Gerald Liebert and Claudia and John
  Ryan
Telephone: 413-528-2720
Rooms: 12, all with private bath
Rates: $46 to $55 per person MAP, double occupancy.
Facilities: Open all year. Breakfast, dinner, full license. Reser-
  vations a must. Pool, and close by are golf, tennis,
  skiing, both downhill and cross-country. Tanglewood
  and Jacob's Pillow are at hand.

Barbara and Claudia, mother and daughter, are the
chefs in this lovely inn. They give you a choice of three
entrees each evening, and all are cooked fresh. The summer
vegetable garden is a 50' × 90' spread of delights. I am sure a
lot of the produce is preserved for winter use. The breads,
pies, muffins and cakes are all ☛ homemade. The dining
room features Currier and Ives snow scenes on the walls and
a ☛ coffee pot bubbling on the mantel all day. Late afternoon you have your choice of tea or cocktail time with a
great assortment of hors d'oeuvres.

The rooms are spacious, all with a private bath, and many with a fireplace.

A game room offers choices of chess, cribbage, backgammon, scrabble and jigsaw puzzles. The living room, full of good early American antques, is comfortable.

There is so much to do in this area it is hard to recount it all. Golf is across the street. The inn's own pool is very relaxing, and in summer you have Tanglewood and Jacob's Pillow near by.

How to get there: The inn is on Route 23 three miles west of Great Barrington.

E: *Gerald moved his grandmother's kitchen table down here from the Tulip Tree Inn in Vermont that they owned. He needs it to knead his good French bread on.*

Our sympathy for the hardships
of our forbears should be somewhat mitigated
by the fact that they had the best
of country inns.

Country Inn
Harwichport, Massachusetts
02646

Innkeepers: David and Kathleen Van Gelder
Telephone: 617-432-2769
Rooms: Seven, all with private bath.
Rates: $30 to $35 double occupancy.
Facilities: Breakfast for house guests, no lunch. Dinner by reservation for transients. Lounge bar and a private dining room for small parties. Tennis, pool, beaches nearby.

The Country Inn is what its name implies, a lovely old Cape home on six acres, covered with rambling roses. Centrally located on the Cape, it makes a great home base for exploring this wonderful part of the world, with its great shopping for just about everything.

The dining room is open to the public for dinner and offers a varied menu, from French and Italian dishes to the more traditional New England fare. All meals include absolutely delicious  homemade cranberry, lemon, and pumpkin breads. Fish specials include escalloped oysters baked in heavy cream, and ocean-fresh haddock, baked, or baked and stuffed. From fish you can turn to chicken Cape Cod with cranberry-spice glaze, chicken cordon bleu or filet mignon. The perfect ending is homemade apple crumb pie with homemade cinnamon ice cream. To make your meal complete they have a choice of five unusually spirited coffees.

Breakfasts are special fun. The normal eggs and omelets are all done differently, which with their homemade breads make the whole meal a delight. The inn has 11 fireplaces. Three are in use downstairs. The rest are in the bedrooms and are lovely to look at, but unfortunately cannot be used.

How to get there: Take Route 6 to Exit 10. Go right on Route 124 (Pleasant Lake Avenue). Cross Main Street in Harwich and continue on Routes 124 and 39 (Sisson Road) to the inn.

E: *The inn was once the guest house on the estate of one of the founders of the Jordan Marsh Company.*

The time between sunset and the completeness of night should be spent around a well laid board with assurances of a warm bed to follow.

olive Metcalf

The Candle Light Inn
Lenox, Massachusetts
01240

Innkeepers: Lynne and James DeMayo
Telephone: 413-637-1555
Rooms: Six, all with private bath.
Rates: $35 to $65 EP, double occupancy.
Facilities: Closed Tuesdays in winter. Open all year. Lunch, dinner and bar. Chef-owned. Downstairs weekends and summer there is entertainment.

Christmas is a time of royal splendor here at the inn. They decorate for each season, but Christmas is just something special and worth a trip from anywhere.

There is an old wagon and an old, double sled on the lawn, Tiffany lamps on the porch, and a lovely flower cart in the entrance hall. Straight ahead is the bar, and what a bar, done pub-style with some of the ☛ greatest stemware I have ever seen.

The dessert cart sits at the entrance of one of the dining rooms with a beautiful array of all ☛ homemade desserts, each one better than the next. There is a gracious fireplace in this dining room. Napery is bluest white. The chairs are comfortable, and the food divine. All the food is fresh and cooked to order; nothing frozen in this chef's kitchen except the ice cubes. The hors d'oeuvres list is more than ample, with four different kinds of clams, shrimp and oysters, in addition to my favorite, garlicky escargots.

Entrees are interesting. At lunch do try the chicken pot pie. It is deliciously different. Dinner entrees like shrimp, crabmeat and scallops mornay en casserole are a delight. Stuffed crepes, or one of the chicken dishes, tempt me to try eating everything on the menu.

The chef-owner, Jim, cooks only with copper utensils, and the food is even served from copper. ☛ Fresh strawberries are served here almost every month of the year.

Flowers are all over the inn, with Boston ferns at the windows, and fuchsias in abundance, usually hanging together with impatiens. And the backyard in summer is a wealth of blooms.

How to get there: The inn is at 53 Walker Street. Turn into Lenox on Route 7-A, off Route 7.

Ô Ô Ô

E: *The small bar with the gleaming stemware is just a great way to end a day*

olive Metcalf

The Inn at Foxhollow
Lenox, Massachusetts
01240

Innkeeper: Donald Altshuler
Telephone: 413-637-2000
Rooms: 41, 20 with private bath, 16 with hall baths, two
  suites.
Rates: $45 to $89, EP, per room; MAP available at $22.50 per
  person, per night, with a minimum two-night stay.
Facilities: Open all year. Breakfast, lunch, dinner, bar. TV,
  billiards, 4,000-volume library, golf, tennis, swimming,
  sailing, yoga, riding, arts center, theater, music, 285
  acres with trails.

The Center at Foxhollow is mind-boggling. There are so
many things to do. The inn itself, all alone, is terrific. Do you
want to walk, eat, and sleep where once trod Vanderbilts and
Westinghouses? Or live in Edith Wharton's house, read
some of her own books? Come to Foxhollow. Drive up the
curving drive lined with ancient pines, leave the world behind and live as the millionaires did when our world was
young. Everyone should have a chance at it once. The Van-

derbilt suite in the main house has a lovely porch with a view of the mountains. Incidentally, the beds are all new, and good.

The former gatehouse, and two gatehouses called Katydid and Cricket, have been transformed into guest accommodations, if the Manor House isn't quite your style.

Here you are, right in the Berkshires, and Tanglewood with its glorious music is just up the road. Right on the estate there are stables, a lake where you can sail, and 14 miles of wandering trails that are also useful in winter for cross-country skiing. Bring the youngsters, for there is so much to do they will never be bored.

The people at Foxhollow have a slightly different approach to innkeeping. They want to give their guests the freedom to discover themselves by doing new things, so there are discussion groups under the stately trees, an art center, even yoga. In their own words: "At Foxhollow we are dedicated to the growth of people. Our purpose is to create an environment where you can expand your awareness of yourself through participation." Foxhollow is different from other places you might go, but all the expected things are here, and of course, in abundance.

How to get there: The inn is located on Route 7, south of Lenox. Take Exit 2 (Lee) from the Massachusetts Turnpike, then take Route 20 north and turn left onto 7.

E: *Crafty lady that I am, the art center beckons me when I am at Foxhollow.*

Olive Metcalf

Three Gables Inn
Lenox, Massachusetts
01240

Innkeepers: Ellen and John O'Hearn
Telephone: 413-637-3416
Rooms: Seven, two with private bath.
Rates: $30 to $55, EP, winter; $40 to $75, EP, summer.
Facilities: Open all year, dining room closed Mondays in winter. Breakfast, continental for guests in winter, and full breakfast in summer. Lunch, dinner, bar.

The inn was once the home of Mrs. Nancy Wharton, mother-in-law of famed author and Lenox resident, Edith Wharton. The author and her husband spent several summers in this house, then known as Pine Acre.

Marble-topped cocktail tables are in the lounge, together with a really neat corner fireplace. Oft times you may meet the father of the innkeeper, who tends bar when he visits. Now I must give equal time to ☞ Mr. Gables, the inn cat with six toes per foot. He is gray with a white mustache. He also keeps the bar, for he sleeps under it.

Ellen plays the harp, and she *is* good. When they need

her, she plays with the Boston Symphony. She gave us an evening of ▄▀ jazz, and until you have heard jazz played, and played well, on a harp you cannot believe how great it is. Of course she also does classical music and handles Rogers and Hammerstein better than a Broadway orchestra. Hearing her is sheer delight.

Food here is interesting, with good appetizers, nice salads, and tasty soups. Dinner is delightfully not expensive in today's world. There are neat crepes of all kinds, and for dessert we recommend you try the Gables Inn Special.

The rooms are adequate. There are fireplaces all over the inn, and if you want to have a meeting there is a good function room that seats 180 people.

How to get there: Off Route 7, going either north or south, take Route 7A. The inn is at the junction of 7A and Route 183. It is 103 Walker Street.

♎

E: *There is so much to do in this lovely town of Lenox anytime of the year.*

Man has tendencies of many temperatures,
the warmest of which is hospitality.

The Village Inn
Lenox, Massachusetts
01240

Innkeepers: Richard and Marie Judd
Telephone: 413-637-0020
Rooms: 25 rooms, 16 baths.
Rates: $25 to $75 EP.
Facilities: Open all year. Breakfast, lunch and brunch, bar.
Parking. TV.

Twenty-five years as an insurance man in New York City has prepared Richard Judd for running a country inn. He really *cares* about people. The 200-year-old house has been operated as an inn for about 150 years. If these old walls could talk . . . . Hand-hewn trees of stout size, fastened with wooden pegs, support its roofs and floors. The inn has been done in all colonial wallpaper, and one long hall has photographs of all our presidents, which is quite a sight. The attics abound with ancient trunks, valises and dusty hat boxes filled with antique possessions of guests, innkeepers, and their employees. Come for a night, a month, or the rest of your life. There is a cordial welcome for music lovers, antique seekers, and country inn buffs.

☞ Poor Richard's Pub was built in the old cellars, and is furnished with seats made from church pews, stained glass, a wall aquarium, and a tool collection from the past. It opens at 11:30 a.m. (1:30 on Sunday) to serve drinks and hot sandwiches until very late evening. There is a cozy corner for lovers, and in winter a bright fire will warm your bones.

Breakfast is very special. Anyone who serves eggs Benedict and champagne gets my applause. Lunch, the only other meal served here, is also a winner. Super salads and overstuffed sandwiches are but a few of the selections on the menu. Both meals are served on the screened porch in summer.

There's so much to do in this quaint old town, and near it. Not far away is the studio of the great sculptor, Daniel Chester French, who did the Lincoln Memorial in Washington, D.C. The Williamstown Theater and the Clark Art Museum are a short drive up Route 7. Norman Rockwell's collected works can be seen in the Corner House Museum in nearby Stockbridge. The dance at Jacob's Pillow and classical music at Tanglewood, just a mile down the road, are world famous.

How to get there: It takes three hours by car from New York, via the Taconic Parkway, and two hours from Boston, taking Exit 2 from the Massachusetts Pike. Or try a Greyhound or Bonanza bus, which will stop around the corner from the inn.

E: *Poor Richard's Pub is my place, and this is the only inn I know that serves Irish Coffee for breakfast every day.*

olive Metcalf

Wheatleigh
Lenox, Massachusetts
01240

Innkeeper: A. David Weisgal
Telephone: 413-637-0610
Rooms: 16 summer, 15 winter, all with bath.
Rates: $85 to $125 double occupancy in summer; $110 to $125, MAP, double occupancy in winter.
Facilities: Closed first three weeks in November. Breakfast for house guests, lunch in summer, guests only, dinner, bar. Swimming, tennis, golf, horseback riding, trout fishing, ice skating, and skiing all nearby. Parking.

Looking for a villa in the hills near Florence, Italy? Seek no more. Here at home in our beloved Berkshires is the most romantic inn in New England. An American contessa dwelled here at the turn of the century. Now it is owned by David Weisgal, who runs it with the help of Florence Brooks-Dumay. This indomitable couple dusted off the cobwebs, used gallons of white paint, and yards upon yards of ☞ white, dotted Swiss for the canopied beds, then scraped and repolished acres of floors . . . and opened for business.

Patios, porticos, pergolas and terraces surround this lovely old mansion. The carvings over the fireplaces, all cupids entwined in garlands, are exquisite. The view of the Stockbridge Bowl, a lovely little lake, is beautiful. Do you long for your own balcony? Reserve one here. And perhaps the nicest touch of all is that you are right on the doorstep of the famous Tanglewood Music Festival. In summer do be sure to make reservations well in advance, as the Festival draws visitors from all over the country.

Walk down to the Poodle Tower, once used as the water storage tower of the mansion, and look for the 20 little gravestones which mark the final resting places of the Contessa's little dogs.

In summer a screened-in pergola is a delight for lunch. The dining room is gracious unto its age, with hanging plants at all the arched windows, a beautiful rug, and excellent food. The chef is justly famous for his homemade pecan pie. Your diet should be left at home in the drawer.

How to get there: Take Route 7 to Stockbridge. At The Red Lion Inn, where Route 7 turns right, go *straight* on Prospect Hill Road, bearing left past the lake and Music Inn, and uphill to Wheatleigh, with its entrance on the right. By car from New Jersey, take the New York Thruway to the Berkshire Spur Exit, which leads to the Massachusetts Turnpike. Continue to the Lee Exit. Follow signs into Lenox. In the center of Lenox, at the Curtis Hotel corner, turn left on Stockbridge Road and go to the bottom of the hill. Then turn right and continue about 1½ miles, keeping left for the Wheatleigh entrance.

E: *The Tiffany windows beside the grand staircase are the most exquisite things I have ever seen. Pale pastel, and curving. How in the world did he do it?*

Olive Metcalf

Jared Coffin House
Nantucket, Massachusetts
02554

Innkeeper: Philip Whitney Read
Telephone: 617-228-2400
Rooms: 46; 12 in main house, 16 simpler rooms in Eben Allen
Wing, 12 rooms in the Daniel Webster House across the
patio, and six rooms in the Federalist House.
Rates: $50 to $75 double occupancy, EP, per room.
Facilities: Open all year. Dining room, Eben Allen Room for
private parties, The Tap Room, and the patio for summer
luncheon. Breakfast, lunch and dinner.

It's well worth the 30-mile trip by ferry, or a plane trip
from Boston or New York, to end your journey at the Jared
Coffin House in Nantucket. Built as a private home in 1845,
the three-story brick house with its slate roof became an inn
only 12 years later. In 1961 the Nantucket Historic Trust
purchased the house, and two years were spent restoring the
main building, the addition, and the adjoining house, to their
original style and architecture. Nantucket Island has become
the center for a revival of needlework that is unprecedented

anywhere in the country, and perhaps the world. ☛ Six thousand yards of material were made to decorate the guest rooms of the Jared Coffin House. The spirit and feeling of the glorious days of Nantucket's brief reign as queen of the world's whaling ports remain in the lovely inn.

☛ The Tap Room, located on the lowest level, is a warm, happy room. The main dining room, papered with authentic period paper, is quiet and elegant. Wedgewood china and pistol-handled silverware reflect the good life demanded by the nineteenth century owners of the great whaling ships.

The inn is located in the heart of Nantucket's Historic District, only an eighth of a mile from a public beach, and a mile from the *largest* public beach and tennis courts. It's a pleasant three-mile bicycle ride from superb surf swimming on the South Shore.

How to get there: Take the ferry from Woods Hole, but first call 617-540-2022 for reservations. There is a summer ferry from Hyannis, too. Or take a plane from Boston, Hyannis or New York. The House is located two blocks north of Main Street, and two blocks west of Steamboat Wharf.

E: *The size and the quantity of the luxurious bath towels pleased me greatly. The housekeeping staff does a wonderful job, and the exquisite antiques reflect their loving care.*

Snug in a country inn, I have finally found the perfect topping to a windy Cape Cod day.

olive Metcalf

Country Inn at Princeton
Princeton, Massachusetts
01541

Innkeepers: Don and Maxine Plumridge
Telephone: (617) 464-2030
Rooms: Six parlour suites, each with private bath.
Rates: $79 to $99, double occupancy, with continental breakfast.
Facilities: Open all year. Closed Mondays and Tuesdays. Dinner served Wednesday through Sunday. Sunday brunch 11 a.m. until 2 p.m. Credit cards accepted are American Express, MasterCard, and VISA.

"The year 1890 had a way about it," says this inn's brochure, and they are so right. The inn is a ☛ Victorian delight. It was built with meticulous attention to every detail by Charles G. Washburn, an industrialist and outspoken senator, and a close friend of Theodore Roosevelt.

The parlour is exquisite with original, slowly whirling, Casa Blanca ceiling fans, plus Victorian chairs and couches that are beautifully upholstered and very comfortable. All through the inn you will find ☞ greenery displayed with fine taste.

There are three elegant dining rooms. The red room is a private party spot for up to 12 people. There is the garden room and the main dining room, on whose ceiling are five Casa Blanca fans. From the gracious windows you have a distant view of Boston's twinkling lights at night.

Cuisine is continental French and excellent. The menu changes every six weeks. Don and Maxine have put their good business experience to work by finding two chefs worthy of their aims for creating an inn with the best food in New England. Chris Woodward is the head chef and Wayne Gorenson is the second. Together they make magic. One of the entrees I had was ☞ Salmon en Croute, fresh filets stuffed with a mousse of tender scallops and watercress, all wrapped in puff pastry and served with a butter sauce and lemon. Do try it.

The accommodations are six extremely ☞ spacious parlour suites. They are sumptuous. Each one is different, and I could live forever in any one of them.

How to get there: From just north of Worcester on Route 290 take Route 140 north to Route 62, turn left to Princeton. When you reach the blinker by the post office turn right, and the inn is on your right just up the hill.

E: *By now you all know I am an animal nut, and so are Don and Maxine. Reno is a doberman, and a real pussy cat. Crystal is a magnificent umbrella cockatoo, Goose is the cockatiel, and Poncho is a yellow naped Amazon parrot.*

olive Metcalf

The Red Lion Inn
Stockbridge, Massachusetts
01262

Innkeeper: Betsy Holtzinger
Telephone: 413-298-5545
Rooms: 110, 80 with private bath. Six suites in summer, two in winter.
Rates: $30 to $70 winter; $36 to $104 summer, double occupancy.
Facilities: Open all year. Breakfast, lunch, dinner, bar, swimming pool, outdoor patio. Elevator in summer. Ramps for the handicapped. Pink Kitty Gift Shop.

The Red Lion Inn is a four-season inn. In summer you have the Berkshire Music Festival at Tanglewood and the Jacobs Pillow Dance Festival, both world renowned. The inn's own ☞ heated swimming pool is a nice attraction. Fall's foliage is perhaps the most spectacular in New England; in winter there are snow-covered hills, and in spring come the lovely green and flowers. All go together to make this a great spot anytime of year.

The inn is full of lovely old antiques. The halls are lined

with antique couches, each one prettier than the next. From a four-poster, canopied bed to beds with great brass headboards, all the rooms are marvelously furnished and comfortable as sin. Whether in the inn itself or in one of the inn's two adjacent places, Stafford House and Ma Bucks, you will love the accommodations. ☛ The wallpaper in Ma Bucks is a delight. All rooms have ☛ extra pillows, which I love.

☛ Excellent food is served in the lovely dining room, or if you prefer, in the Widow Bingham's Tavern. There is an almost-hidden booth in here designed for lovers.

The Lion's Den is downstairs with entertainment nightly, and it has its own small menu. In warm weather the flower-laden courtyard with its Back of the Bank Bar is a delightful place for food and grog.

Blantyre, for those of you who know it, has been purchased by The Red Lion Inn adding 14 more guest rooms. This is a grand place for an elegant party.

How to get there: Take Exit 2 from the Massachusetts Turnpike and Route 7 north to the inn.

E: *Norman Rockwell lived in Stockbridge. The Corner House is a step down the street, so do not miss this great museum of this wonderful artist's works.*

olive Metcalf

Colonel Ebenezer Crafts Inn
Fiske Hill, Sturbridge, Massachusetts
01566

Innkeeper: Pat Bibeau
Telephone: 617-347-3313
Rooms: 10, all with bath.
Rates: $42 to $80, EPB, double occupancy.
Facilities: Open all year. Continental breakfast for guests, afternoon tea, small swimming pool.

In colonial times the finest homes were usually found on the highest points of land. Such a location afforded the owners commanding views of their farmland and cattle. It also set them above their contemporaries. So David Fiske, Esquire, a builder, built this house in 1786 high above Sturbridge. The house has been magnificently restored by the management of the Publick House, and they have named it after that inn's founder, Colonel Ebenezer Crafts.

The bedrooms are large, full of good antiques and period reproductions, and offer sweeping views of the surrounding Massachusetts hills.

Patricia Bibeau, the innkeeper, will greet you when you

arrive and give you a tour of the house, but do remember to ask to see a bit of the underground railway of Civil War days. The slave hole is still here. These old homes certainly do take you back in time.

 Fresh baked muffins, juice and coffee for breakfast, come along with a copy of the morning paper. Tea and sweets are served in the afternoon, and fruits and cookies are on your night table. To make things just right, you will find your covers neatly folded back.

When you are ready for some real good food, go two miles down to the famous Publick House in Sturbridge. There you will find some of the best food this side of heaven, including those always present sticky buns.

How to get there: Take Exit 3 from I-86, and bear right along the service road into Sturbridge. Continue to Route 131, where you turn right. Turn left at Hall Road and then right on Whittemore Road, which becomes Fiske Hill Road.

E: *Buddy Adler, the innkeeper at Publick House, is justifiably proud of this beautiful old house.*

There is no definition of a proper inn.
Like night and day it either is or is not.

olive Metcalf

Publick House
Sturbridge, Massachusetts
01566

Innkeeper: Buddy Adler
Telephone: 617-347-3313
Rooms: 21 rooms, air conditioned, all with private bath. An additional facility, 1⅓ miles from the Publick House, is the Colonel Ebenezer Crafts House, with nine rooms, swimming pool and complimentary continental breakfast.
Rates: $38 to $80.
Facilities: Open all year. Direct dial telephones in every room. Breakfast, lunch, dinner, bar. TV in the lounge. No elevator, but there is a ramp to the restaurant. Gift shop.

Very little has changed at the Publick House in the last 200 years. The green still stretches along in front of it, and the trees still cast their welcome shade. Not far away, Old Sturbridge Village has been assembled and restored, a living museum of the past. The Publick House is still taking care of the wayfarer, feeding him well, providing a bed, and supplying robust drink. Many of the old practices and celebrations have been revived here. The Boar's Head Procession during the Christmas holiday is one. They *do* keep Christmas at the Publick House! All twelve days of it. ☛ Winter weekends are times for special treats, with chestnuts roasting by an open fire, and sleigh rides through Old Sturbridge Village, a happy step backward in time.

Twenty-one guest rooms have been decorated with period furniture, and the wide floor boards and beamed ceilings have been here since Colonel Ebenezer Crafts founded the inn in 1771. The barn, connected to the main house with a ramp, has been transformed into a restaurant. Double doors, topped by a glorious sunburst window, lead into a restaurant that serves delectable goodies. There is a little musician's gallery overlooking the main dining room that is still divided into stalls. Beneath this is an attractive taproom, where a pianist holds forth, tinkling out nice noises.

A blueberry patch, and a garden which covers more than an acre of land, provide the inn with fresh fruit and vegetables during the summer.

I found my way by following my nose around behind the inn to the Bake Shop, where every day fresh banana bread, sticky-buns, deep-dish apple pies, corn bread, and muffins come out of the ovens to tempt me from my diet! Take some along, for hunger pangs along the road.

How to get there: Take the Massachusetts Turnpike to Exit 9. The Publick House is located on the Common at Sturbridge, on Route 131. From Hartford, take I-84. It becomes I-86, and brings you right into Sturbridge. Take Exit 3.

E: *Way on top of the inn is a suite called the Penthouse. The view from these rooms in the very early spring, with all the feathery new leaves, is enough to bring me back from the far corners of the earth.*

Longfellow's Wayside Inn
Sudbury, Massachusetts
01776

Innkeeper: Francis J. Koppeis
Telephone: 617-443-8846
Rooms: 10 air-conditioned rooms, with private bath.
Rates: $25 single to $30 double, per room.
Facilities: Closed on Christmas, open year-round. Telephones in nine of the 10 rooms. Dining room. Breakfast, lunch, dinner, and bar. Horses boarded. Pets limited. No room service or TV.

Eight generations of travellers have found food and lodging for "man and beast" at the Wayside Inn. Route 20 is the old stagecoach road to Boston, now well off the beaten track. You will find the inn looking much the same as it has for over 270 years, still dispensing hearty food and drink, and supplying a few comfortable beds. In early times people on the road slept five or six to a room, but now the rooms with twin beds and private baths are limited to two.

In 1955 the inn was partially destroyed by fire, but the older part was saved, and when the restoration was done many things were put back the way they were in the beginning. Many of the nineteenth century "improvements" were changed. Part of the inn serves as a museum, with priceless antiques displayed in their original setting.

There is a large dining room, a bar, a tiny gift shop, and a lovely, walled garden. At the end of the garden path is a bust of Henry Wadsworth Longfellow, who was inspired by the inn to link together a group of poems in the fashion of The Canterbury Tales. The Landlord's tale is known to us all as Paul Revere's Ride.

Henry Ford bought 5000 acres surrounding the inn in 1925, and since then this historic spot has been preserved for generations yet to come. A little way up the road stands a lovely chapel, the little red schoolhouse that gained fame in "Mary Had a Little Lamb," and a stone grist mill that still grinds grain for the rolls and muffins baked at the inn. ☛ In the summer vegetables served at the inn are locally grown.

How to get there: From Boston take the Massachusetts Pike to Route 128, north to Route 20, Exit 49 west. Coming from New York, take the Massachusetts Pike to Route 495, to Route 20, east.

E: *The waterfall at the grist mill really flipped me. The stone work is unbelievable!*

Olive Metcalf

The Westbridge Inn
West Stockbridge, Massachusetts
01266

Innkeeper: Henricus Bergmans
Telephone: 413-232-7770
Rooms: 10, one with private bath.
Rates: $24 to $32, double occupancy.
Facilities: Closed the week before Thanksgiving and Mondays
and Tuesdays in the winter. Continental breakfast for
house guests, bar, lunch and dinner.

Henry has been an innkeeper for a long time, and he
knows how to do it right. The inn was built in 1804. I will talk
about the food rather than the rooms, though they are
adequate.

There is a stained-glass panel behind the bar and a pair
of Victorian lamps on either side of it, a wonderful sight.

A potbellied stove at one end of the bar sure felt good
the night I was there. Lunch and dinner are served in this
room and in the more formal soft, blue dining room, by
candlelight of course.

The menus are presented on artists' easels. This makes

for good conversation at the table while everyone discusses the dishes. There is at least one special entree served each night along with the regular fare, which includes things like lamb chops, roast duck à l'orange, chicken, veal, fish and a yummy Yankee pot roast. The soups are rich and delicious. One of the appetizers I tried was ☛ mussels in a garlic wine sauce. Mussels never tasted better. The desserts are ☛ homemade pies and cheesecake, plain or with fresh strawberries, and good, good, good.

Henricus is an innkeeper's innkeeper. It's fun to be with a man who does things so well.

How to get there: West Stockbridge is the last exit on the Massachusetts Turnpike going west. The inn is on Main Street right in town.

𝄞

E: *Four beers on tap, Tuborg Gold, Miller, Miller Lite, and Michelob, are a fine way to quench a thirst.*

Olive Metcalf

The Victorian Inn
Whitinsville, Massachusetts
01588

Innkeeper: Martha Flint
Telephone: 617-234-2500
Rooms: Eight, six with private bath.
Rates: $45 to $67.
Facilities: Open all year. Dining room for lunch Tuesday through Friday. Dinner everyday except Monday.

This wonderful Victorian house, built in 1871, has been treated kindly through the years. One owner (there have been only three) moved in, decided to go to Paris for a vacation, and was so sick on the boat going over that he never came home. Instead he stayed in Paris 41 years and died there. Fortunately, he had a caretaker, and the house survived. So several years later when Martha Flint began searching for a country inn to buy, she came here. ☛ Food is the name of the game here, and there are three dining rooms, the Library, the elegant drawing room, and the original dining room. Beautifully served and deliciously different, there are 12 dinner entrees, some purely classic and others deliciously unique. Desserts are mind-boggling, and there are exotic coffees, too. Our Victorian forebears should have had it so good.

The rooms are delightful, huge, furnished in a style to match the house. The hand-tooled leather wainscoting in one of them is a marvel, and one of the bedrooms has its original wallpaper. Martha not only has a flair for food, she also is an exceptionally gifted decorator. The picture wall in the little dining room is fair testimony.

How to get there: Take Exit 11 from the Massachusetts Pike (I-90) to 122 south. Turn right at the sign to the business center. Go through town to the large intersection, turn left onto Linwood Avenue, and you will see the inn, on the left, after 1½ miles. Or, from Rhode Island, come north on Route 146 and look for a blinking yellow light with signs for Uxbridge Center, which you follow, leaving 146. You will come to a stop sign in front of the Cock and Kettle Restaurant. Follow Route 122 north through two traffic lights. Linwood Avenue is the next left after the second light. Turn left to Whitinsville and you will see the Depot Lounge, and the inn is just around the corner.

E: *The menu cards, circa 1924, bring a charming touch of Art Deco into this lovely inn.*

Le Jardin
Williamstown, Massachusetts
01267

Innkeeper: Walter Hayn
Telephone: 413-458-8032
Rooms: Nine, eight with private bath.
Rates: $32.50 to $42.50 per room including continental breakfast.
Facilities: Closed Tuesdays only from November to May. Lunch, dinner, bar, Sunday brunch.

Hemlock Brook burbles past the sugar maples from which Walter makes ☞ his own maple syrup. In early spring each tree is festooned with old-fashioned sap pots, and in the kitchen there is a huge pot boiling it all down.

The old-fashioned rooms have all been renovated to make your stay more than comfortable. One of the rooms, and my favorite, has a canopied bed and a fireplace.

The menu is excellent. There are ☞ four different salad choices at lunch, and this to me is ideal. Of course there are sandwiches and hot selections also. The dinner menu is more than a little French, though nicely translated into the language of the country. The essence of good food is time, but even the hasty diner is taken care of here with good steaks and chops. The hors d'oeuvres are sinful. The quiche is a gruyere cheese custard pie. I adore garlic and the escargots are a garlic lover's dream come true. The entrees are deliciously different, including filet of sole topped with spinach and glazed with a classic, delicate white cream sauce, or chicken with mushrooms in light wine cream sauce inside a pastry shell that is light as a feather. The steak tartare, I learn from a reliable source, is the best ever. Desserts are something else. I can remember sitting at the bar talking with Walter while he plied me with three different calorie laden desserts he had just made.

The bar is delightful, with comfortable bar stools, tables, an old piano, and most important, a red setter who really runs the inn. His name is Strider.

How to get there: The inn is right on Route 7, just two miles south of Williamstown on the right.

E: *Terry Perry is manager of the dining room. She does a superb job.*

Who can refuse the beckoning
of a cozy country inn?

Olive Metcalf

The Colonial House Inn
Yarmouth Port, Massachusetts
02675

Innkeeper: Malcolm J. Perna
Telephone: 617-362-4348
Rooms: 12, all with private baths.
Rates: $35 double occupancy MAP winter, $45 double occupancy EPB.
Facilities: Open all year. Expanded continental breakfast (but no eggs), lunch, dinner, bar.

This was a lovely old sea captain's home, and now is a lovely old country inn serving some very fine food. At lunch, the day I was there, the Quiche du Jour was eggplant and the Crepe du Jour was chicken. I had to have a taste of both and they were excellent. I also had ☛ lobster salad that was superb, not all overdressed with dressing but done just right. The chef also whips up a different cheese dip daily for your crackers.

The dinner menu with beautiful treats from the sea, Tournedos Rossini, steaks, and chicken is a joy. Meals are beautifully served in one of three intimate dining rooms. The

Oak Room is so named because there are 10 different kinds of oak in here. The Colonial Room has hand stencilled walls, and the Common Room is a glass-enclosed veranda with a view of the garden and a lovely waterfall and fountain.

The rooms are furnished with antiques, comfortable beds and tons of charm. All have private baths.

This is a very comfortable place to be, shady old oaks and spacious lawns, a rocker on the porch and good food, plus all the delights of The Cape right at your doorstep. What more can one ask for.

How to get there: Leave Route 6 (the mid-Cape highway) at Exit 7 and go north to Route 6-A. Turn right and about one and one-quarter miles, midway between Willow and Union streets, on your right is the inn.

ᵍ

E: *Malcolm, our innkeeper, just makes you feel so at home.*

*Well cooked, well served, and well eaten,
a meal at a good country inn.*

Old Yarmouth Inn
Yarmouth Port, Massachusetts
02675

Innkeeper: Shane E. Peros
Telephone: 617-362-3191
Rooms: 12, all with private bath.
Rates: Inquire for seasonal rates.
Facilities: Closed on Mondays, November 1 to May 1. Lunch, dinner, and bar. Parking. TV. Continental breakfast for house guests. Open all year for lodging.

The Old Yarmouth Inn is the oldest inn on Cape Cod. Built in 1696 as a Wayside Staging Inn, it has had many owners, but it maintains its charm. The building sags a bit, and when you come in it is like savoring a bit of yesterday, with old leather suitcases, quaint papered hat boxes, dusty coats, hobnail boots, and ancient horse brasses, all combining to carry you back to the olden days.

There is salt air here, flowers, sunshine, somedays a little fog. You can dine indoors or out at the Old Yarmouth Inn, and seafood is, of course, a specialty of the house.

Vegetables, salads, and herbs come fresh from the garden; flaky pastries, rich cakes, and hot breads burst from the ovens.

You are only four miles from the famous Cape Playhouse at Dennis, one of the original "straw hat" theaters. There are several fine beaches nearby, and fishing, boating and day trips to Nantucket and Martha's Vineyard can be arranged.

How to get there: Leave Route 6 (Mid-Cape Highway) at the Yarmouth Port Exit to Route 6A. Turn right, and one mile will bring you to the Old Yarmouth Inn.

E: *The antique bug is gonna bite me, sure's I live, if I keep coming back to Yarmouth Port.*

The aroma of freshly baking bread told me surely I was awakening in a good country inn.

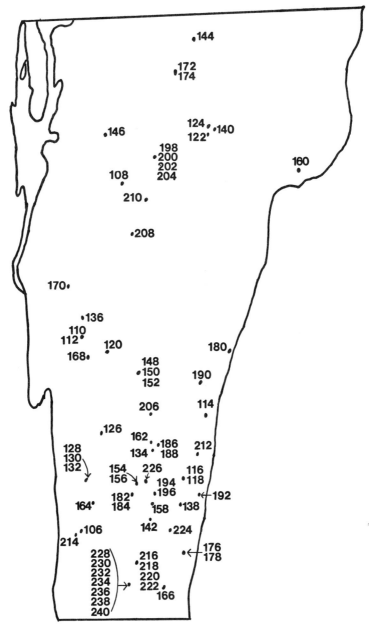

numbers on map refer to page numbers in this book

Vermont

Olive Metcalf

West Mountain Inn
Arlington, Vermont
05250

Innkeepers: Mary Ann and Wes Carlson
Telephone: 802-375-6516
Rooms: 11, some with private bath; housekeeping facilities.
Rates: $25 to $35, EP.
Facilities: Open year-round. Breakfast, dinner, bar. James
    Walker Stoneware Studio in the stable barn. Hiking
    and cross-country ski trails, fishing and swimming in
    the Battenkill River.

This inn is truly in the country, on a mountainside
overlooking the village of Arlington, with 150 acres of trees,
trails, pastures, and ponds. Cross the trout-filled Battenkill
River, wind your way over the bridge, which is flower-laden
in summer, go by the millhouse, up past the main cottage
and spring-fed rock quarry, to the seven-gabled inn. ☛ The
grounds around the inn are reputed to have more species of
evergreens than any place in New England. There are lovely
trails for hiking, jogging, or cross-country skiing, depending
on the season.

The inn is filled with a unique "family." Mary loves to cook fresh vegetables from her kitchen garden. Jim will let you throw some clay on the wheel in his stoneware studio in the stable barn. Amie and Willie, the Carlson's children, will introduce you to the goats, Goose and Gander and Duck; and Frodo, their Dachshund. Wes loves to show off his African violets and exotic goldfish, and there are visiting artists who share their talents with the guests. The beauty of the natural setting, the warm environment of the inn, with its plants and quilted beds, make you come away relaxed, refreshed, and revitalized.

Old George, an *enormous* trout, inhabits the secluded pond, encouraging anglers to try their luck. He has to be over 24 inches long!

How to get there: Midway between Bennington and Manchester, Vermont, exactly a half mile west on Route 313, off Route 7, turn onto River Road. Cross the river and go up the hill until you come to the inn.

⧗

E: *The enthusiasm, the smiles on everyone's faces at this charming inn warm my heart.*

The Black Bear
Bolton Valley, Vermont
05477

Innkeepers: Erik and Grace Stavrand
Telephone: 802-434-2126
Rooms: 20 rooms, all with private bath.
Rates: $35 to $44 double occupancy, per room. I do suggest you write for rates, as they have MAP and EP weekends.
Facilities: Closed April 15 to May 15, and all November. Heated pool, tennis, skiing, bar.

This is a perfect place, winter or summer, for a family vacation. There are inn children, not too much in evidence, though you might be able to catch a glimpse of them berrying along the road. The inn is set up for families. Grace, your hostess, is also the cook. Wholesome, uncomplicated American food is what you will find here. ☛ The mountain view from the flower-filled balconies is superb. You are minutes from the Bolton Valley Ski Area, and there is also tennis and horseback riding available.

The highlight of your stay may well be the candlelit

dinner served by the fireside, ☞ and what a fireside it is! There is a small bar, if this is your pleasure, and since dinner is for house guests only, there is lots of time for leisurely conversation. This is another country inn that has that special quality of a private house.

This area is just too grand to miss, and remember, you can take Amtrak trains to Waterbury Station, and buses to Burlington, Jonesville, or Waterbury. Or fly right into Burlington, but do come up.

How to get there: From Burlington, go east on I-89. Take Exit 11 at Bolton-Richmond. Continue east on Route 2 for eight miles, through Richmond and Jonesville. Turn left onto Bolton Valley Road in Bolton, where I-89 passes over U.S. Route 2. Four miles up Bolton Valley Road, and you are at the Bear.

From Montpelier, go west on I-89, and take Exit 10 at Stowe-Waterbury. Turn left off the exit ramp and cross I-89. Then turn right onto Bolton Valley Road in Bolton, where I-89 passes over U.S. Route 2. Four miles up Bolton Valley Road, and you are at the Bear.

♧

E: *The sunny, yellow counters in Grace's sparkling new kitchen brighten our lives.*

olive Metcalf

The Brandon Inn
Brandon, Vermont
05733

Innkeepers: Trudy and Al Mitroff, and family
Telephone: 802-247-5766
Rooms: 60, 48 with private bath, others with connecting
    bath. All sprinkler protected.
Rates: $42 to $55 per person MAP.
Facilities: Open all year. Breakfast, lunch, dinner, bar. Ele-
    vator, ample parking. 40 air-conditioned rooms, TV,
    swimming pool.

Your host at the Brandon Inn, famed as a hostelry since
1786, finds no language barrier with his guests; ☛ Al
Mitroff speaks *nine* languages! This charming Czech-born
innkeeper brings a continental flavor to an old colonial inn.
More than 40 years ago he was a busboy at the old Waldorf-
Astoria, from there he went to the St. Regis, and thence to
the 1939 World's Fair in New York. Although he already had
a degree in Physical Education from Columbia, he also went
to Cornell to learn the hotel business. It is a *pleasure* to stay at
the Brandon Inn.

The rooms are large. They originally weren't large enough to suit our host, so he made one large room where two were before. These rooms in the back of the inn used to be used by the coachmen and are prized today for being away from the road. The public rooms are charming, and there are ☞ two enormous Pier mirrors in the old parlor that must be priceless.

With a filtered, crystal-clear swimming pool, shuffle board court, chip-and-putt green, croquet area, fishing brook with an old mill dam, and a summer theatre on the grounds, this inn provides the guest with a great melange of things to do. There are easy and interesting walks around the inn, and four golf courses are but a five to 20-minute drive away. Nine major downhill ski areas are within a 10 to 45-minute drive, and two cross-country ski areas are 10 minutes away.

The gardens behind the inn, and the swimming pool, are lovely. The food is good, served by friendly ladies. ☞ When the wine we chose proved to be unavailable, Al Mitroff came himself with an especially chosen bottle for our pleasure. ☞ The inn has been enshrined in the distinguished Historic Sites Register.

How to get there: Brandon is located on U.S. Route 7 and Vermont Route 73, on the village green 16 miles north of Rutland. It is 3½ hours from Boston, 5¼ from NYC, and three from Montreal. Greyhound and Vermont Rapid Transit buses stop in Brandon; there is air service to Burlington or Rutland; Amtrak trains go to Essex Junction and White River Junction.

E: No two rooms are alike, so I can go 60 times. ·

Churchill House Inn
Brandon, Vermont
05733

Innkeepers: Mike and Marion Shonstrom
Telephone: 802-247-3300
Rooms: 11, six with private baths.
Rates: $38 to $45 per person MAP.
Facilities: Closed mid-March to mid-May and mid-October to mid-December. Breakfast and dinner. Lunch (winter only) of soup and fresh-baked French bread. Canoeing, fly-fishing, inn-to-inn skiing, hiking, and bicycling tours.

This really is an inn for everyone, a good family inn because from here you can do it all. You can hike along a 60 mile section of Vermont's Long Trail. Each day's adventure ends at another inn for lodging and meals. A car shuttle takes care of your luggage and your car. You need only go as far as you care to. The same goes for the ski touring and the bicycle tours. Do write them for their folders on all these tours, plus a special on fly fishing for native trout. These streams are not crowded with other anglers. Mike has assured me the rainbows are large and sometimes huge. Sound like a fish story? Better come on up and see for yourself.

The inn is an 1871 New England farm house. There are six wood-burning stoves to warm the cockles of your heart and feet. The bedrooms are all furnished with antique, high bedsteads of maple, oak or brass. Real comfort for a tired hiker or skier, even a winded bicycler.

Marion has a huge garden. She uses fresh vegetables in the summer and her own things frozen or canned in the winter. She makes all her own bread and desserts. She considers herself an international cook and proves it with a wide variety of good foods.

How to get there: From Rutland follow Route 7 north to Brandon. Turn right on Route 73. The inn is on your left.

♏

E: *The inn is the Churchill Inn. The inn cat, of course, is Winston.*

*A day by the fire, a hot ale in hand
and the idiot cares of the world are as nothing.*

olive Metcalf

The Inn at Mount Ascutney
Brownsville, Vermont
05037

Innkeepers: Eric and Margaret Rothchild
Telephone: 802-484-7725
Rooms: Six, three with private bath.
Rates: $33 to $42, EPB, double occupancy; $28 to $35 single.
Facilities: Closed April and November. Breakfast for house
  guests. Dinner, bar, skiing, summer theater. Dinner is
  served Thursday through Monday.

A country inn that serves 🐾 tea at four in the afternoon reminds me of jolly old England. Margaret is a
🐾 Cordon Bleu chef, and the inn features country cooking
with a continental flair. The kitchen where Margaret works
is part of the dining room, so you watch this fine chef at
work.

The dining room and lounge were converted from an
old carriage house, and they still have the old beams and an
open hearth. There is a small dining room for small con-
ferences or special parties. A small room overlooking the
meadows is reserved for breakfasts.

The inn is located directly across the valley from the Mount Ascutney ski area. In winter you can sit in the inn and watch the skiers, which is 🐾 quite a sight at night when the lights are on.

I love inn animals, and here we have a few of them; two cats, Sherlock and Pink, and one dog, Chivas.

Whether a skier or summer walker, this inn is a great spot for a few days to rub off the tussel and trials of everyday life.

How to get there: Take Exit 8 from I-91 northbound, or Exit 9 southbound. Then take Route 5 to Windsor, and go left on Route 44. The inn will be on your right.

E: *I am a choc-a-holic, and Margaret's own creation is called* 🐾 *Chocolate Mount Ascutney. Need I say more. Delicious.*

*The snow could pile as deep as a mountain
with no worry for me, for I was in the tavern
of a friendly country inn.*

Olive Metcalf

Chester Inn
Chester, Vermont
05143

Innkeepers: Tom and Betsy Guido
Telephone: 802-875-2444
Rooms: 35, with baths.
Rates: In season $24 to $30 per person, double occupancy,
   EPB. Off season $21 to $28 per person, double occu-
   pancy, EPB.
Facilities: Closed last three weeks in April, and first two weeks
   in November. Breakfast for house guests. Dining room
   closed Monday. Lunch Tuesday through Saturday. Bar.

When you arrive in Chester, you will find the Chester
Inn gracing the Village Green. Walk up the steps onto the
large porch with rocking chairs, and on through the door to
the spacious living room with fireplace and great comfortable furniture. To the left, scout out the real ☛ English pub.
Pass through the door to the pool and patio area outside.
Then pick a favorite spot, and rest a bit.
   Some golden October day you might find a covey of
antique cars parked in front of the inn. They don't come

every year, so check with the innkeeper about them if this is your hobby.

There are seven skiing areas nearby, so for the skier who likes to ski a different area each day of the week, this is the logical place to lodge. After a day on the slopes, return to the inn for a drink in the pub, a gourmet dinner, and then go off to a snug bed. What more could you want? On Saturdays there is even a piano player for entertainment.

The spacious dining room has so much charm, and the heated swimming pool and two, new, all-weather tennis courts provide plenty of opportunity to exercise after that delicious gourmet dinner.

How to get there: From I-91 take Route 103 to Chester. The inn is on Route 11 on the Green.

E: *There is a shop connected to the inn called "The Golden Pheasant," run by a very charming lady.*

The dog nuzzled my leg. The fire sent out a glow.
The drink was good. Only at an inn.

Cranberry Inn
Chester, Vermont
05143

Innkeepers: Barbara and Michael Yusko
Telephone: 802-875-2525
Rooms: 11, four with bath, others share.
Rates: $31 to $33, EP, per room.
Facilities: Closed in April. Breakfast and dinner served to house guests. Room and restaurant accessible to wheelchairs. Private parties.

Traveling down Route 11 one beautiful day I came upon this lovely old inn, a haven for anyone who wants to retreat to the country. Beams abound, and every room has been freshly redecorated.

There is skiing everywhere around here, and when you come back all cold and rosy from an outdoor day you will be greeted with ☛ a warm fire from a wood burning stove, and pots of steaming, homemade soup. For this I would get cold.

Mike Yusko used to come up here from New Jersey to ski. Now he and Barbara have come to stay, and are making the Cranberry Inn a must on any list of New England inns.

Your stay here promises to be a memorable one in any month or season. Spring and summer offer fishing, horseback riding on forest trails, and the wild colors of autumn can be enjoyed from your car, or afoot, or even from your bike. November brings the hunters, and then snow covers every peak and valley. Ski cross-country, or enjoy the slopes at Magic Mountain, Stratton, Bromley, Okemo, Ascutney, Round Top, Killington, or Pico.

How to get there: Turn off I-91 onto Route 103. Follow it to Chester and take Route 11 west to the inn, which is on the right.

E: *Cranberry glass has long been one of my favorite things. I share my enthusiasm for it with Barbara.*

The good morning greeting and the goodnight good wish can only be found in a country inn.

olive Metcalf

Mountain Top Inn
Chittenden, Vermont
05737

Innkeeper: Wm. P. Wolfe
Telephone: 802-483-2311
Rooms: 36, all with private bath.
Rates: $100 to $120 MAP, double occupancy. $65 to $100 MAP, single occupancy.
Facilities: Closed March 31 to May 31 and mid-October to mid-December. Open for conventions during closed periods. Breakfast, lunch and dinner, bar and lounge. Heated pool, lake recreation, tennis, badminton, croquet, shuffleboard, pitch 'n putt, sauna, and game room.

This is one of the most beautiful inns in New England. The views are breathtaking. At a 2,000-foot elevation the inn overlooks Mountain Top Lake, which is surrounded by fantastic mountains.

Everything is here, including crackling fireplaces, sauna, whirlpool, and the great-and-only ☛ "Charlie James" Cocktail Lounge, presided over by a regal fox. There is a spectacular ☞ two-story stairway of glass and natural cherry wood leading down to the lower level, where you will find the dining room and cocktail lounge. Food served here is truly gourmet, with Seafood a l'Indienne, a blend of seafood in a tangly curry sauce with chutney; or braised, boneless chicken breast in honey, rum and pineapple; or crisp duck, lamb chops, and much more. And all so very good.

The rooms, most overlooking the lake and mountains, are large and luxuriously furnished, with ☞ king, double or twin beds, and all with spacious baths. A nice touch is your bed turned down at night with a maple sugar candy on your pillow.

Here at the inn they have an excellent ski touring program. To go with it is the old horse barn, where you can relax around antique stoves, sip hot apple cider, and discuss cross-country skiing.

There is ample room for all, with the inn's more than 500 acres. This, with the adjacent National Forest land, gives you 55 miles of scenic trails meandering through mountains that are as beautiful to walk as they are to ski.

The inn has ski-sleds, toboggans, and an ice skating area, and you alpine skiers are but 20 minutes or less from the Pico and Killington slopes.

How to get there: On Route 7 at the north edge of Rutland turn east onto Route 4. In about three miles turn left on Mountain Top Road, cross the bridge and go straight up the hill 1.8 miles to the inn.

E: ☞ *Sleighs drawn by ponies or horses are a wonderful yesteryear experience.*

The Craftsbury Inn
Craftsbury, Vermont
05826

Innkeepers: Perley and Carol Fielders
Telephone: 802-586-2848
Rooms: Nine, two with full bath, two with a half bath.
Rates: $55 to $65 MAP, double occupancy.
Facilities: Closed October 15 to January 1. Restaurant closed on Monday. Breakfast for house guests, dinner, bar. Parking. Swimming, tennis, golf, fishing, riding, skiing, all nearby.

The inn is a lovingly restored Greek Revival house that was built around 1850. The little town of Craftsbury, said by the *Boston Globe* to be Vermont's most remarkable hill town, was founded in 1788 by Colonel Ebenezer Crafts and lies in what is called The Northeast Kingdom. The population today is something less than 700. That includes Craftsbury, East Craftsbury, and Craftsbury Common.

Perley and Carol Fielders came north from our nation's capital to reopen this beautiful old house. Perley is a native Vermonter, an inspired chef, and when the inn is closed he takes off to Europe to study wines and great cuisine.

The ice creams are all freshly churned, and the French breads and pastries are baked right here. The Lamb Chops with Tomatoes Provencale are different, as is the Roast Duckling with elderberry and ginger sauce. This is just a small sampling of the excellent food served up here.

What's to do in Craftsbury? Rent a canoe from a man who makes them up at the Common. Play golf on Vermont's oldest golf course, hilly enough for a mountain goat, in nearby Greensboro. Play tennis, go fishing, sit on the veranda and read, swim in any of four nearby lakes, take a walk, take a hike, go shopping, look at the leaves in fall, ski in winter. Unwind, relax, or discover the rural delights of the tiny towns with all their auctions, antiques and collectibles everywhere.

During July and August the Craftsbury Chamber Players perform every Thursday evening. Make plans to go.

How to get there: Take I-91 to St. Johnsbury, pick up Route 2 west, and at West Danville take Route 15 to Hardwick. Follow Route 14 north to Craftsbury. The inn is on the right, across from the general store.

E: *The fireplace in the living room is the original fireplace that warmed the first post office in Montpelier, Vermont's capital. The main portion of the inn is heated by an oil-steam furnace that came into being in 1802 and was finally patented in 1899. It is believed to be the oldest working furnace in northern Vermont, and most likely, the entire state.*

Olive Metcalf

The Inn on the Common
Craftsbury Common, Vermont
05827

Innkeepers: Penny and Michael Schmitt
Telephone: 802-586-9619
Rooms: 12 guest rooms, three with private bath, two rooms
with fireplace above the craft shop, across the street.
Rates: $40 to $45, MAP, double occupancy. $25 to $40 EPB.
Facilities: Closed in November and April. Food and drinks
served to house guests only. Tennis, croquet, boating,
swimming pool, cross-country skiing, backgammon.
Ski touring and ski packages. Will open off season for
private parties.

If there aren't too many of you, come to The Inn on the
Common. It has grown a little, since Penny and Michael
Schmitt bought the house directly across the street and
added some rooms above ☛ the loveliest craft shop in all
New England. The delectable meals are served in a beautiful
dining room at two lovely big tables, under the solemn eyes
of two genuine ancestral portraits. Names are provided upon
request.

Fresh vegetables and herbs come from Penny's own garden, her imaginative use of things like sorrel and basil give meals a definitely different flavor. I hope you'll be here some evening when caviar eggs are on the menu. Your hostess loves to surprise the most sophisticated of diners. You can always get a good piece of beef, fresh brook and rainbow trout caught by local fishermen, and "wild turkey," grain-fed nearby. Six different salad dressings make even the most dedicated salad detester cry for more.

Craftsbury Common is one of the loveliest villages in New England. It was founded in 1789, and many of the buildings date to the late eighteenth and early nineteenth centuries. The gardens in this town are fabulous, including the inn's very own. The Schmitts also have a 150-acre farm in nearby Greensboro, where you can go for nature walks.

The excellent clay tennis court has the most breath-taking view of the Black River Valley and the mountains beyond; a wonderful place for Sam, the inn dog, to live.

How to get there: Follow I-91 to St. Johnsbury, take Route 2 west, and at West Danville take Route 15 to Hardwick. Take Route 14 north to Craftsbury, and continue north into the common. The inn is on the left as you enter the village.

E: *The solar-heated swimming pool, new last year, has a dark painted bottom, flagstone edges, and a little waterfall to let the water in. It disturbs nothing in its peaceful location behind the Common Market.*

olive Metcalf

Shrewsbury Inn
Cuttingsville, Vermont
05738

Innkeepers: Lois and Don Butler, Gil and Kerry Dillon
Telephone: 802-492-3355
Rooms: Six, all share a nest of bathrooms.
Rates: $18 per person EP.
Facilities: Closed mid-April to mid-May and November. Breakfast, lunch June through October. Dinner Tuesday through Saturday. Sunday brunch summer only. Pub lounge. Skiing nearby.

Lois Butler should have been an interior decorator. She has done such a fantastic job with this marvelous country inn. ☛ All in the family is the theme here. Son, Gil, is the chef. Son, Kerry, is the pub keeper and all around builder and fixer. Daughter, Pat, is waitress, breakfast chef, bread baker and creative soft sculpture maker. All under one roof. Wow!

Chef Gil does different things with food. Good examples are ☛ Chicken Livers Marsala or chicken breast Dijonnaise. ☛ Scotch eggs are an unbelievable appetizer and so is a dessert which is honest-to-goodness old fashioned strawberry shortcake. Remember this is only a sample of what they have.

Kerry's pub is delightful. In one permanent seat sits Agnes Cornpepper, a life size soft sculpture by daughter Pat. No need to ever drink alone here. Agnes is at hand. Wine labels cover the bar and are also on the ceiling above the chandelier.

The living room is just as inviting. Lois has done a superb job. She is a medieval buff. Son Gil's wedding was in medieval costumes all created right here and beautiful. They hang about the inn. One dining room is small and formal, and the other is a grand medieval one with a large table that seats six.

Only six bedrooms so do reserve ahead. Each room is done better than the next. They are large, airy and beautifully done.

This truly is an inn creeper's (as I am known) delight.

How to get there: North on I-91 to Exit 6 and north on Route 103 to Cuttingsville or north on Route 7, right on Route 140 in Wallingford and left on Route 103. The inn is on your left just short of the village.

E: *Mr. Finnegan is the inn cat who looks and acts like one I once had. He has his own ☛ needlepoint sign on the front door telling whether he is in or out. Some class!*

Olive Metcalf

Barrows House
Dorset, Vermont
05251

Innkeepers: Charles and Marilyn Schubert
Telephone: 802-867-4455
Rooms: 28, all with private bath.
Rates: $50 to $110 MAP, double occupancy.
Facilities: Closed the first two weeks in November. Breakfast,
    lunch in July, August, September and October. Dinner,
    tavern. Parking, TV, ski-touring, fishing, hunting, out-
    door heated swimming pool, two outdoor tennis courts,
    golf, sauna.

Barrows House has been here a long long time, and the welcome is still old-fashioned and warm. Winter sports are enhanced by the thought of a sauna when you return. Charlie and Marilyn Schubert are young, vigorous, attractive, and fun. Charlie was in public relations and Marilyn was an airline stewardess, and if that doesn't give them a running start on being innkeepers, I don't know what does. The bar is a lively spot for the local residents, as well as travellers.

The Schuberts have a lot of ski-touring equipment, and this new version of an old sport is most popular here.

The menu is lovely, and in summer the ☛ fresh vegetables are unusually prepared. Sauteed cucumbers in dill, and zucchini with peppers and onions, are two excellent dishes. The selections change with what is fresh at the moment. Whatever the season, Barrows House will be ready for you, and after all, how many inns can you find that will turn down your bed at night?

After a hearty breakfast, the innkeepers will ☛ outfit you right down to your picnic lunch and give you a gentle shove onto a door-front trail, from which you may share a memorable day with the Vermont countryside. Ritz, the inn dog, may tag along.

How to get there: Take Exit 2, in Brattleboro, from I-91. It is marked Manchester, Route 30. Follow Route 30 for one hour, through Manchester to the Barrows House. Or take Route 7 to Manchester Center, then go north on Route 30.

🍐

E: *This one is high on my preferred list and should be popular with golfers, as the Dorset Field Club extends golfing privileges to inn guests.*

olive Metcalf

Dorset Inn
Dorset, Vermont
05251

Innkeeper: Fred G. Russell
Telephone: 802-867-5500
Rooms: 45, almost all with private bath.
Rates: $26 to $30, MAP, per person, double occupancy.
Facilities: Closed October to Christmas, and mid-March to late May. Breakfast, lunch, dinner, bar. Parking. TV. Wheelchair accessibility to dining room.

This is the oldest inn in Vermont, and it has been continuously operated as an inn. There is nothing antique about the welcome you receive, however. The Dorset Field Club, sporting one of Vermont's oldest nine-hole golf courses, extends golf privileges to guests of the inn. Summer or winter, this is a fine place to stay. There are ☞ Wednesday night cookouts that everyone looks forward to.

If culture turns you on, the Southern Vermont Arts Center and the Dorset Playhouse will provide the comedy and drama of good theater. In summer, swim in the beautiful pool at the inn, go boating on Emerald Lake, or go horseback riding over old, forgotten roads, and past stone fences.

☛ Bicycle touring is an especially enjoyable enterprise at this lovely inn, with many groups staying the weekends for the fresh air and exercise.

There is all sorts of great skiing within easy driving distance of the inn, and as many places, "Ski Weeks" and "Ski Weekends" are featured here, with late-arrival snacks, apres-ski fondue, hot wine punch, and popcorn.

How to get there: Leave I-91 at Brattleboro, take Route 100 north to Londonderry, and go left on Route 30 to Dorset. Or take Route 7 to Manchester Center, and go north on Route 30.

E: *A few years ago, before I ever thought I would be involved in this book, I stayed here while skiing. The inn is as lovely now as it was then.*

*When you have but one night to spend
which inn to choose is as difficult as
the choice you had years ago at the
penny candy counter, and equally rewarding.*

olive Metcalf

Village Auberge
Dorset, Vermont
05251

Innkeepers: Alex and Hanneke Koks
Telephone: 802-867-5715
Rooms: Four, two suites, all with private bath.
Rates: Winter, $37.50 and up MAP; summer, rooms only,
$35 to $50.
Facilities: Closed April 15 to May 15, and November 15 to
December 15. In summer closed Mondays, and in win-
ter closed Mondays and Tuesdays. Breakfast and
dinner, skiing, Cornucopia Antique Shop.

Stained-glass windows are always lovely, and the one
that separates the bar from the dining room is especially
well done. Hanneke is an interior decorator and fashion
designer by profession. ☞ The inn reflects her talents.
The dining room is just beautiful. It seats only 45 people
and is done in shades of warm green. The stunning place
plates are a floral pattern from Villeroy and Boch, and Botan-
ica made in Luxembourg. Needless to say the food served
here is extravagant, with hors d'oeuvres and potages such as

prosciutto and stewed prune relish, cream of mustard soup, and my love, escargots in garlic butter. There is always a special of the day and many more entrees, from veal, steak, sweetbreads and lamb, to fish of the season. Ready for dessert? You must come and taste for yourself and leave your calorie counter in your desk.

The bar is done in rich, warm wood, and is a beauty. The rooms are lovely. The one suite is spacious. There is a fireplace in the lounge.

The innkeepers are extremely experienced. Alex attended hotel management school in The Hague, and he has owned and operated restaurants in Haarlem, Holland and Marlboro, Vermont. Hanneke, along with her other talents, operates a unique antique shop right on the inn property.

There is much to do in this area. Three downhill ski areas, cross-country skiing, and the Dorset Playhouse are less than a walk around the block from the inn. Nearby are tennis, golf, and swimming.

How to get there: Leave I-91 at Brattleboro and take Route 100 north to Londonderry, then go left on Route 30 to Dorset.

♡

E: *I have a special fondness for bay windows, and the dining room has a beauty.*

Old Town Farm Lodge
Gassetts, Vermont
05144

Innkeepers: Fred and Jan Baldwin
Telephone: 802-875-2346
Rooms: Ten, two with private bath.
Rates: $30 to $34, MAP, per person, double occupancy.
Facilities: Closed on Thanksgiving and Christmas. Breakfast,
   dinner. No bar, BYOB. Parking.

If you like to ski and you have youngsters, throw every-thing in the car and head for the Old Town Farm Lodge. There are four young Baldwins already in residence. Simple, hearty meals are served with one main course. The Lodge is located ☛ in the heart of 11 ski areas, and the Baldwins can direct you to where the skiing is best. Nearby there is hunting, fishing, hiking, golf, swimming, and riding. They have it all, and without the swinging nightlife enjoyed by the singles crowd.

The lodge is busiest during the foliage season, so be sure to reserve ahead if you are going leaf peeping. The Baldwins are busy all year, restoring, rebuilding, replacing the farm house that is over 100 years old. It was once known as The Town Farm, because the indigent of the neighborhood were given food and lodging here, in return for a hard day's work. Vermont Maple Syrup is served exclusively, of course.

 Cycle Inn Vermont is a bicycle touring service put together by a few Vermont inns, Old Town being one of them. This is a wonderful way to see New England, and also to stay at a different inn each night. Your luggage is transported by car for you.

How to get there: Gassetts is five miles north of Chester Depot on Route 10.

E: *The handmade spiral staircase that curves to the second floor is so beautiful, and it has been painstakingly restored to its original condition.*

Were it not for a night's rest in a country inn
tomorrow would be but another day.

olive Metcalf

Blueberry Hill
Goshen, Vermont
05733

Innkeepers: Martha and Tony Clark
Telephone: 802-247-6735
Rooms: Eight, all with private baths.
Rates: Summer $47 per person MAP, winter $55 per person
MAP.
Facilities: Closed mid-March to mid-May and November.
Breakfast, in summer a pack lunch and in winter a soup
lunch in the ski shop, dinner. BYOB. Rental and retail
ski shop, instructions, tours, hiking and running.

The inn is a cross-country skiers dream come true
perched high up in the Green Monutains with good clean air
and well groomed, snowy trails. The inn has its own ☛ ski
rental and retail shop along with good instructions. Night
skiing is fun, and so are all of the other tours that the inn
provides. The ski trails are used for hiking, walking or running in the summer. There is a pond for swimming and
streams and lakes for fishing.
The meals are family style served around a large table

and prepared by Martha who is a fine gourmet cook. All of her ☞ baking is done right here. I found a basket of cookies fresh and warm and so good, just waiting for a hand to pick one up. You cannot eat just one unless you have a will of iron. Martha has a large garden, and she does her own canning and preserving for the long winters.

The family room has a huge fireplace, and all over the inn you will find Martha's ☞ upside down gardens hanging from the ceiling beams, a colorful and imaginative use of straw flowers Martha has plucked from her own gardens.

The greenhouse off the kitchen is unique. The doors to some of the bedrooms are in here. It is warm, sunny, full of plants and a wonderful spot for your morning coffee.

There are plenty of books to read, and the rooms are all comfortable with many antiques. There are special home-made quilts to warm you.

Buttermilk is the inn cat and Sniff is the inn dog. He will go right along with you on your tours.

How to get there: From Rutland take Route 7 north to Brandon, then Route 73 east for six miles. At the inn sign turn left. Follow the inn signs up the mountain on a dirt road to the inn.

E: *Martha's* ☞ *ever bubbling soup on the old pot belly stove tastes grand after a day's touring.*

olive Metcalf

The Old Tavern
Grafton, Vermont
05146

Innkeeper: Lois M. Copping
Telephone: 802-843-2375
Rooms: 35, all with private bath. Four houses.
Rates: $35 to $65, EP, single or double occupancy.
Facilities: Closed in April, on Christmas Eve and Christmas
Day. Breakfast, lunch, dinner, bar. Swimming, tennis,
nature walks. TV in lounge, parking, elevator.

Over the hills and far away is a Vermont village called
Grafton. The Old Tavern here has been operated as an inn
since 1801. Since 1965, when the inn was purchased by the
Windham Foundation, it has been restored and is now one of
those superb New England inns we all are seeking.
When you turn your car off pounding interstate highways to the tree-shaded route that winds to this quaint
village, you do step back in time. The loveliest of the old,
combined with the comfort of the new, makes this an un-
beatable inn. No grinding motors can disturb your slumber
when you are in ☛ the best beds in all New England. The

sheets and towels are the finest money can buy, there are extra pillows and blankets in each room. The spacious rooms are filled with antiques, all in mint condition.

There is no "organized activity" at the Old Tavern. ☞ The swimming pool is a natural pond, cool and refreshing. There are tennis courts nearby, and marked trails in the woods for walkers. This is the place to calm your spirits, recharge your batteries.

The cocktail barn is charming, connected to the inn by a covered walk. There are flowers everywhere, hanging in baskets, in flower boxes, and on various tables in the gracious public rooms. The food is excellent, with unusual soups, varied entrees, all cooked well, and served by pleasant waitresses.

☞ Up the street a ways there is a six-box stall stable that will accommodate guest horses, plus a four-bay carriage shed, if you care to bring your own carriage. All this for the exclusive use of Old Tavern guests.

How to get there: Take Exit 5 from I-91, at Bellows Falls, and go to Route 121, which comes before you negotiate the entire exit ramp, so keep out a sharp eye.

E: *The houses across the street that are also part of the inn are enchanting.*

Highland Lodge
Greensboro, Vermont
05841

Innkeepers: Willie and David Smith
Telephone: 802-533-2647
Rooms: 11, all with private bath; eight have double and twin
   beds. 11 cottages.
Rates: $70, MAP, single; $70 to $80, double occupancy.
Facilities: Closed April 1 to May 25, and after foliage until
   December 20. Breakfast and dinner. Beer and wine
   license only, setups are available. Parking. Swimming
   and boating on Caspian Lake, tennis.

Highland Lodge is really the place to get away from it all. With peace and quiet, delicious home-cooked meals, and the delightful Smith family, you can recharge your batteries for life easily. But don't mistake us, there is lots to do here in Greensboro. ☛ Caspian Lake, with the lodge's own beach house, is just across the road, with swimming, canoeing, sailing, and fishing. Tennis, golf, and riding are available for those inclined.

People come back year after year to this friendly place.

There are book-lined walls, puzzles to while away a long afternoon, but mostly, a good mix of genuine, real, down-home folksiness. It comes over you as soon as you walk through the door. There is a "recreation house" with supervised play for the youngsters, so a stay here can be a real vacation for parents.

In the fall this is one of the great spots for foliage, and it isn't far to the White Mountains, or the Green Mountains. And cross-country skiing in winter is a newfound delight in this unspoiled country. This area is personally recommended by my publisher, who used to summer in Greensboro. The rooms are decorated beautifully and are very comfortable.

How to get there: Greensboro is 35 miles northeast of Montpelier, Vermont. Take I-91 to Route 5 north to St. Johnsbury, and follow Route 2 west out of town. At Danville take Route 15, turn right on Route 16, which will bring you into Greensboro. Go left out of town, and keep left. Caspian Lake is on your left, and the inn is on the right side of the road.

E: *The new winter recreation room out back is great for the younger set.*

"Drink wine, and live here blitheful while ye may;
The morrow's life too late is, live to-day."
—Herrick

olive Metcalf

Three Mountain Inn
Jamaica, Vermont
05343

Innkeepers: Charles and Elaine Murray
Telephone: 802-874-4140
Rooms: Eight, six with private bath. One housekeeping cottage available by the week.
Rates: $17.50, EP, per person; to $45, MAP, per person.
Facilities: Closed April 15 to May 15. Breakfast and dinner, pub, lounge. Skiing, tennis, swimming pool.

The inn is well named, since it is within a few minutes of Stratton, Bromley, and Magic Mountains. Mount Snow is also within easy range. Skiers should love its location. Cross-country buffs will find a multitude of trails at the inn's doorstep, including a 🐄 dramatic trail along the long defunct West River Railroad bed.

This small, authentic country inn was built in the 1780's. The living room has a large, roaring fireplace, complete with an original Dutch oven. The floors and walls are of wide, planked pine, and authentic. There are plenty of comfortable chairs, and a picture window offering views of the

Green Mountains to complete the scene.

A cozy lounge and bar area with a piano make you feel very comfortable for sitting back to enjoy good conversation and a before or after dinner drink. ☞ A good wine selection is at hand.

The rooms are tastefully decorated. One room has a large, four-poster, king-sized bed in it. Another has a private balcony overlooking the swimming pool and garden.

Dinners are a special treat. The menu changes frequently, though you always can be assured of the freshest meats, fish, and vegetables available. Breads, soups, and desserts are all homemade. There are three dining rooms, one with a library, and dinner is always a candlelight affair.

How to get there: Follow I-91 to Brattleboro and take the second exit to Route 30, to Jamaica.

ಠ

E: *There are guided tours for fly fishermen on the West and Battenkill rivers. Write for these package deals, and remember you will eat what you catch.*

*If you have never been drawn shivering
from the warmth of a good bed
by the sizzling lure of bacon on the grill,
you have never been in a country inn.*

Jay Village Inn
Jay, Vermont
05859

Innkeepers: Patricia and Bill Schug
Telephone: 802-988-2643
Rooms: 14, 10 with private bath.
Rates: $33 per person, MAP.
Facilities: Closed mid-April to late May. Breakfast and lunch on weekends, dinner, bar. TV in lounge, swimming pool, alpine and cross-country skiing. Ski and sport shop.

When you get to Jay, Vermont, you are nearly in Canada, so this makes the Jay Barn Inn our most northern Vermont inn. Nestled at the foot of Jay Peak, this little place is a delightful country inn. Come any time of year, the Fireplace Lounge and Bar is noted for its apres-ski and evening pleasures. Sip a ☛ hot buttered rum and enjoy the flaming fire and player piano while you socialize with friends, old and new.

The inn is well-known for its American and continental cuisine, served in the Galerie d'Art Dining Room. You will

144

find lots of paintings, antiques, and objets d'art here, inspired by Patricia and her family from France. They add a light European touch to this delightful inn.

If you are a skier, you must know that Jay Peak has one of the longest, most dependable ski seasons in the East. The Aerial Tramway is a "trip," and there are exciting trails for the beginner as well as the expert.

There are two golf courses in the vicinity, if that's your thing, and if you are a hiker you are close to the Long Trail. Summer days, all too few of them, can be spent in complete idleness at the pool, or the more ambitious can bike or hike, for northern Vermont is beautiful. The inn is just across the road from the Jay Country Store, and there is a ski and sport shop called Snow Job right at the inn.

How to get there: Take Route 100 up to Troy, turn left on Route 101, and three miles later turn left onto Route 242 for about one mile to the inn.

🕯🕯🕯

E: *The quaint, quiet bar with its huge stone fireplace is the warmest place on the coldest day.*

*A night at an inn adds a tinge to the coming day
that cannot be described, only enjoyed.*

The Windridge Inn
Jeffersonville, Vermont
05464

Innkeeper: Alden Bryan
Telephone: 802-644-8281
Rooms: Five, all with bath.
Rates: $30 to $35, EP, double occupancy.
Facilities: Closed on Thanksgiving. Open year-round. Breakfast in the bakery-dairy bar just next door. Lunch at the inn from June 1 to November 1, dinner 6 to 8:30 p.m., year-round. Parking. Skiing, tennis, indoor and out.

Part of this little inn is as old as it looks, and it has that quaint New England charm, from the patchwork quilts on the comfortable twin beds, to the handmade braided rugs.

The name of the game here is tennis, indoor, outdoor, on clay courts, by day or night, but always with a heated lounge and dressing rooms. Of course, you're not all that far from Stowe, either. So the skiing is great, and the inn has some good ski week packages offered, from Sunday evening to Friday morning, except on holiday weeks.

What is really different and engaging about Windridge

Inn is that Salle de Poulet. All across one side of the dining room is long narrow window. There is a slatted blind that pulls across this. When it is open, you are gazing into the homelife of some doves. They are really pretty, and fun to watch.

The luncheon menu is truly inspired, with eggs Benedict, Salade Nicoise, omelets, chipped beef in mushroom wine sauce; and they have Lowenbrau. The dinner menu is also very good, with French-style food, and the famous Windridge breads, baked right here.

How to get there: Jeffersonville is northeast of Burlington. Route 15 from Burlington will bring you right into town. Take Exit 10 from I-89 at Waterbury, then take Route 100 north to Hyde Park. Turn left on Route 15.

*Having had an excellent meal and
a lovely evening, I tucked myself in bed knowing I
had sinned but it did not seem to matter.*

Olive Metcalf

The Inn at Longtrail
Killington, Vermont
05751

Innkeepers: Kyran and Rosemary McGrath
Telephone: 802-775-7181
Rooms: 16, 12 with private bath, six suites.
Rates: Rates vary with season. MAP offered fall and winter.
Facilities: Closed April 15 to June 15, and end of the foliage
season to Thanksgiving. Breakfast and dinner. Lunch in
summer only. TV, bar, music, skiing and hiking.

Music warms my heart, and here at the inn on weekends, during foliage season and sometimes during the week,
you can hear really good ☛ folk and bluegrass music. This
all happens in the pub room, which has a bar 22 feet long and
six inches thick made from a single pine log that was cut just
south of Woodstock, Vermont. They also have a single-seater
bar alongside ☛ the largest boulder I have ever seen inside
a building. It extends 12 feet along the wall and rises right
through the ceiling. The walls are barn wood decorated with
antique tools, photographs and drawings. A wood-burning
stove underlines the total comfort of the room.

In the dining room is more of the great boulder, six feet of it. Another wood-burning stove is here. Seating is for 68 people, all of whom can enjoy the large picture windows looking out at spectacular Vermont scenery.

The living room is a large, wood-paneled room with a huge, stone fireplace and comfortable, handmade furniture. There is a special place on the hooked rug for Tara the inn dog, a black Labrador retriever.

The Appalachian and Long Trails pass alongside the inn, and nearby lakes provide swimming, fishing and boating. The Festival of Arts at Killington offers folk and jazz concerts. The Green Mountain Guild produces excellent summer theater for your pleasure. As for skiing, you are surrounded by it.

The rooms are small and cozy. The suites are neat, with your own fireplace, color TV, studio couches and beds, and of course, a full bath.

How to get there: The inn is east of Rutland on Route 4 at the Sherburne Pass.

E: *The huge boulder is subtly lit at night. Quite a sight.*

Hark, which are common noises
and which are the ghosts of long contented guests.

Mountain Meadows Lodge
Killington, Vermont
05751

Innkeepers: Bill & Joanne Stevens
Telephone: 802-775-1010
Rooms: 15, two small bunk rooms, all but three with private
   bath.
Rates: $25, MAP, per person; EP available.
Facilities: Closed in May. Open every day of the week. Break-
   fast and dinner for house guests, no bar, BYOB. Park-
   ing. TV, skiing, hiking, swimming.

     This is the first inn in the book to be actually on a hiking
trail through the Green Mountains. I have not included all
New England inns in this guide, as some of them are a little
too rustic to get my recommendation. But there are some
that are quite all right, you understand, for hikers.
     You can pick up a brochure here if you want to try
hiking the route on foot. This is a casual family lodge with
110 acres that overlook one of the loveliest lakes in the
mountains.
     Two darling cats own this inn, Pax and Boots, and the

door is guarded by Susqua, a gentle dog who doesn't seem to miss one of his paws. The inn is mostly in the converted barn, built in 1856, and the house is somewhat older. They have the largest ski touring center in the area, right at the lodge. The food is hearty Vermont home-style, served by friendly waitresses.

How to get there: The inn is 10 miles east of Rutland, off Route 4. Follow Route 4 from Rutland for 12 miles, and at Thundering Brook Road you will come to the inn sign. Turn left. The inn is a quarter mile beyond.

E: *It was here that I met Bear, a mostly red setter, who had just come in off the Appalachian Trail carrying his own backpack. True, I swear.*

If all inns were alike they simply would not be inns.

olive Metcalf

The Vermont Inn
Killington, Vermont
05751

Innkeepers: Alan & Judy Carmasin
Telephone: 802-773-9847
Rooms: 14, eight with private bath, six with hall bath.
Rates: In summer, $25 to $35 EPB, per room; in winter, $30
to $40, MAP, per person.
Facilities: Closed in May, and restaurant closed Mondays.
Breakfast for house guests, dinner, bar. TV, game room,
pool, tennis, lawn games, gondola ride, summer the-
ater, cross-country and downhill skiing.

You may be greeted at the door of this friendly red
house by a companionable Labrador named Tammy. Judy
and Alan are always here, and a nicer young couple you'll
have to travel a long way to find. The Vermont Inn is well-
known locally for the fine food served in the new dining
room. There is also a children's menu, a true help for the
traveling family.

The inn guests are a mixed bag. You'll run into young
professional people from Boston or New York, a grandparent

or two, families, anyone from honeymooners to golden oldies. Alan has assembled, or gathered, a fine wine cellar to enhance the good food.

The rooms have all been redecorated. Floors have been recarpeted or painstakingly restored to the original wood. What a labor of love! This old house has sturdy underpinnings. Some of the original beams still have the bark on them, and how the rocks of the foundation were ever put in place I cannot imagine. Everything is still being changed around, the old dining room has fast become a lounge to make the inn cosier, so take advantage of the beautiful view of Killington, Pico, and Little Killington, straight ahead across the valley.

Tammy's "Instructions to Guests" on how she is to be treated should be on the *must* list for every inn dog. They are tacked up at the desk. Drop in and read them, then stay awhile.

How to get there: The inn is east of Rutland, four miles west of the intersection of Route 4 and Route 100.

🍇

E: *The stretched fabric pictures everywhere are so bright and attractive. Old and modern, and all blended together.*

The style is the inn itself.

Nordic Inn
Landgrove, Vermont
05148

Innkeepers: Filippo Pagano and Inger Johansson
Telephone: 802-824-6444
Rooms: Five, three with private bath.
Rates: $37.50 to $46, MAP, per person.
Facilities: Closed April 15 to July 1. Breakfast for house
     guests, lunch in winter, Sunday brunch in summer,
     dinner, bar, skiing, and darts.

Inger Johansson is the chef-owner of this inn. She is
from Kisa, Sweden. While there, she was head chef for the
Consul General of Sweden, which makes for Sweden's loss
and Vermont's gain. This lady is one of the few ☞ gourmet
chefs in our book. The menu is unusual. The food, whether it
is fish, veal, beef, pork, or chicken, ☞ is different, beautifully served, and a joy to eat. Inger also excels in ☞ soups
and super desserts.

Filippo is the bartender, in addition to being a dart
expert, carpenter, and all those other things so necessary to
running a good inn. Filippo has the only ☞ pro dart shop in

Vermont, and probably in New England. Wednesday is dart night, and once a year he holds a "New England Championship" tournament. This all happens in the great cellar pub, where in off-hours a special food menu is provided. There is a lovely fireplace down here also.

The inn is a ski-touring center, with a good ski shop and plenty of rental equipment. There are miles and miles of groomed and marked trails in the next-door Green Mountain National Forest, and all the downhill you can ski is nearby.

Filippo and Inger offer their guests a genuine touch of Scandinavia in Vermont. It fits well with the good, New England inn charm.

The inn cat named Sissy has the most unusual amber-cinnamon eyes I have ever seen on a cat. She shares the inn with a dog, a husky, named Lotta.

How to get there: The inn is between Bromley and Londonderry on Route 11, 14 miles east of Manchester.

E: *Inger made me some of her ☛ Swedish pancakes. They looked like a flower on the plate, surrounding a great scoop of Inger's ☛ homemade Lingonberry Jam and rimmed with fresh whipped cream. Oh my!*

The Village Inn
Landgrove, Vermont
05148

Innkeepers: The Snyders
Telephone: 802-824-6673
Rooms: 20, some with private bath, some with hall bath.
Rates: In winter, $32 to $38 MAP, per person; in summer,
$20 to $25 MAP, per person.
Facilities: Open November 15 to April 15, and July 1 to
October 15. No dinner on Wednesday. Pool, tennis,
nine-hole pitch-n'-putt golf course, cross-country ski-
ing, volleyball, bumper pool, Ping-Pong, table hockey.

There is only one question I have about the Village Inn.
Where's the village? This place sits all alone, way out in the
country. Maybe it was the way I came. The Snyders, cordial
welcoming folks, have a friendly relaxed inn.

The architecture is peculiar to Vermont, with one building built onto another building, onto another. It turns out to
be charming. There are some old rooms, and some new ones,
all spick-and-span and comfortable. The first part of the inn

was built in 1810, and the last additions were made in 1976.

The snows lie heavy around here, and cross-country skiing through the National Forest on miles and miles of marked trails is wonderful. You are only a short trip by car from Bromley, Stratton, Snow Valley, or Okemo. And after a long day of skiing, you can come back to the inn for some fireside relaxation in the Rafter Room Lounge.

Summer brings other delights: a neat swimming pool, a whirlpool spa, two tennis courts that are really *used*, and are fun to watch. Summer theater is near at hand, and there is always riding, and hunting, in season.

How to get there: Via I-91, use Exit 6 at Rockingham. Take Route 103 to Chester, then Route 11 to Londonderry. Continue past the shopping center for approximately a half mile, and turn right on Landgrove Road. Go four miles to the Village of Landgrove. Bear left after crossing the bridge and continue one mile to the inn, on your right.

From Manchester, take Route 11 past Bromley Ski Area, and turn left into Peru Village. At the fork in Peru bear left and continue four miles through the National Forest to the crossroads in Landgrove. Turn left toward Weston, and the inn will be on your right.

E: *Lead me to the bumper pool. I must keep in practice; it's my favorite sport.*

Olive Metcalf

The Highland House
Londonderry, Vermont
05148

Innkeepers: Alan & Margaret Unangst
Telephone: 802-824-3019
Rooms: Seven, three baths. One large cottage for eight.
Rates: $15 to $20, EP.
Facilities: Open all year. Dining room closed Sunday. Breakfast, dinner, no bar, BYOB. Skiing and sight-seeing nearby. Parking for horse, car, or bicycle.

The first guests came to Highland House more than 50 years ago. Alan and Margaret are new to innkeeping, but old-fashioned when it comes to being hospitable. Here at Highland House you will find a combination of good, home-cooked meals, served family-style, so you can sit around the fire with friends after a day in the beautiful Vermont countryside.

A day of touring backroads by car or bicycle, visiting antique shops, playing golf or tennis, hiking in the National Forest, hunting or fishing, can end in complete relaxation back at the inn. ☞ The Franklin stoves in the living room

158

and dining room are practical as well as quaint.

How to get there: Take Exit 2 from I-91 at Brattleboro. Take Route 30 north to Route 100, and the inn is just north of town on Route 100.

E: *Look for the litle antique oak ice box, now located in the dining room. They brought it all the way from Allentown, Pennsylvania.*

Insomnia is almost a blessing if you are in an inn within easy earshot of a country church bell.

Rabbit Hill Inn
Lower Waterford, Vermont
05848

Innkeepers: Eric and Beryl Charlton
Telephone: 802-748-5168
Rooms: 20, all with private bath.
Rates: $28 to $47 EP, double occupancy.
Facilities: Closed four weeks in early spring and after foliage season to Thanksgiving. Breakfast for house guests, lunch, dinner, bar.

There is a sign in the dining room in Gaelic. It means 100,000 welcomes, and these warm, friendly innkeepers mean just that.

The dining room has wide floor boards, a Franklin-type wood stove, and pewter and brass from their own collection. It is bright, airy, and serves fine food. The innkeepers' selection is a nightly dinner special chosen from the best the kitchen can conjure up, which is always a good choice. There are, of course, many other entrees including steak, lamb, veal, fish, and chicken. Do try  breast of chicken Devonshire served with a sauce of tangy orange, honey and vermouth. Delicious!

Bedrooms are large and comfortable. Some have fire-places, canopied beds, love seats, and all face east with a view of the Presidential Range. The porch on the second floor is a special spot for me to just sit, rock and look.

There is a library on the second floor full of good books. Please, when you take a book from this inn, or indeed any inn, send it back when you are finished.

The Briar Patch is the ski shop. It has instructions and rentals. The trails are beautiful, winter or summer, winding along and across Mad Brook with its beautiful waterfalls, then on across pastures and deep into lush, wooded areas.

There is a lot of history up here, and this lovely village is on the most photographed list in Vermont.

How to get there: Take Route 2 east from St. Johnsbury and turn right onto Route 18. Or coming from Route 5, take Route 135 east to Lower Waterford.

E: *Many interesting musicians live nearby, and they wander into the inn to entertain. How nice.*

"*Venite ad me ownes qui stomacho laboratoratis et ego restaurabus vos.*"
"*Come to me all whose stomachs cry out in anquish and I shall restore you.*"

olive Metcalf

The Okemo Inn
Ludlow, Vermont
05149

Innkeeper: Rhinard & Toni Parry
Telephone: 802-228-2031
Rooms: 12, 10 with bath.
Rates: In summer, $23, EP; in winter, $41, MAP, per person.
Facilities: Closed from the end of ski season to June 1. Open
rest of the year. Swimming pool, sauna, honeymoon
suite, brass beds, fireplaces, cross-country ski trails. Golf
packages available.

Two little brown dogs named Fred and Barney welcome you when you arrive at Okemo Inn. Fast on their heels
come the Rhinard Parrys, a couple of hard-working youngsters who have a dear little boy. Their house has been here
since 1810, but there's nothing old-fashioned about the
swimming pool. And ☛ the spacious sauna is the very thing
to take the ache away from the first day of skiing.

Meals are served family-style, and are hearty, home-
cooked, featuring roast beef, ham, turkey, chicken, and if

that fare seems a little plain, how about a little Stroganoff just for variety?

The inn is practically at the foot of Okemo Mountain, a fast-growing, popular place to ski.

The inn has a liquor license, and there is a color TV in the lounge. This seems an ideal spot for a couple, or young family, that loves skiing.

A collection of "necessary china" for bedroom use in times bygone is displayed on the bookshelf in the second floor hall. It's a wonder.

How to get there: Take Exit 6 north from I-91, and follow Route 103 to Ludlow. The inn is located one mile from Okemo Mountain public transportation, which includes Vermont Transit buses, and Amtrak trains to Bellows Falls.

E: The Parrys have an 1896 Edison gramaphone that works.

A night at an inn adds a tinge to the coming day
that cannot be described, only enjoyed.

Olive Metcalf

The Inn at Manchester
Manchester, Vermont
05254

Innkeepers: Harriet and Stan Rosenberg
Telephone: 802-362-1793
Rooms: 11, four with private bath.
Rates: Winter, $21 to $27 per person MAP; summer, $26 to $35 bed and breakfast for two.
Facilities: Closed April and November. Breakfast, dinner, beer and wine license, TV, Ping-Pong, cards, and fireplaces.

When you walk in the door of the inn you may be greeted by the inn dog, a Saint Bernard named Christy. In any case your eyes will light on the beautiful greenery in the bay window of the living room. The inn has been well restored and is full of good antiques. The many fireplaces with comfortable sitting areas surrounding them, and a dining room that has ☛ Tiffany lamps, add up to a warm country inn.

The accommodations are of two types. Bunk rooms and singles are on the third floor, all with carpets and great views.

The regular rooms, a floor below, are extremely clean, some with good, new beds and some with antiques. All are done in bright colors, yellows and blues, with dust ruffles that are color-coordinated. All are very nice.

The food is all homemade, even the breads, and is served family-style. Apple pancakes with local maple syrup can start anyone's day right. When my publisher heard that one of the desserts was apple crisp with ice cream, I had to tie him to his chair.

The inn is conveniently located in the heart of just about everything, with skiing, downhill and cross-country, only minutes away. Summer brings great antiquing, summer theater, specialty craft shops and boutiques. Golf and tennis are within walking distance of the front door. This really is a lovely area.

The new game room has TV, Ping-Pong, card tables, and a warm fireplace. Very nice.

How to get there: The inn is approximately 22 miles north of Bennington, Vermont on Route 7. It is on the left.

E: *The shoulder of Equinox Mountain is out the back door and in autumn is a sight to behold.*

olive Metcalf

Longwood Inn
Marlboro, Vermont
05344

Innkeepers: Tom and Janet Durkin
Telephone: 802-257-1545
Rooms: Nine, seven with private bath.
Rates: $45 to $75, double occupancy.
Facilities: Closed Wednesdays. Breakfast for house guests. Sunday brunch. Lunch during the music festival and the fall foliage season. Bar.

The copper lanterns at the door of this more than 200-year-old inn are worth a visit in themselves. The inn has worn many faces over the years. It was first a dairy farm known as the Five Maples, when milk was eight cents a quart, then a halfway house, a college dormitory, next a local theater, and now an engaging country inn. In the summer there is still ☞ live theater in the red barn, a step across the yard from the house. In nearby Marlboro is the world-renowned music festival each summer.

Any time of year is a good time to come to the Longwood Inn. In winter ski downhill or cross-country at nearby areas, or when the roads are clear, bring your bicycle or rent a horse and see this marvelous area in a more leisurely fashion.

The most important ingredient found at Longwood's restaurant is the restful luxury of dining in leisure. The menu invites you to partake of homemade soups, fresh vegetables, a Caesar salad prepared at your table, fish, beef, chicken or veal. The chef's special is jumbo garlic shrimp sauteed in good, garlicky butter and topped with herbed bread crumbs. Yum, yum. Ask for the special mulled cider or grog in fall and winter. All are creatively prepared. Desserts are delectable, coupes aux marrons, Kahlua cheesecake, and mousse au chocolat. Breakfasts are a bit above the ordinary with home-made muffins, and Wilhelmina blueberry pancakes with pure Vermont maple syrup. Oh my, what a way to go.

How to get there: From I-91 take Exit 2 at Brattleboro. Take Route 9 to Marlboro. The inn is on the right.

🎵

E: *Barnaby, the inn cat, really runs the inn with an iron paw.*

The groaning breakfast board of a good inn
always makes it difficult to remember the word "diet."

Olive Metcalf

Red Clover Inn
Mendon, Vermont
05071

Innkeepers: Dennis and Bonnie Tallagnon
Telephone: 802-775-2290
Rooms: 10, all with private baths.
Rates: $25 to $40, MAP, per person, double occupancy.
Facilities: Closed from mid-October to Thanksgiving, and from April 15 to Memorial Day. Breakfast, dinner, bar. TV, pool, cross-country and downhill skiing, summer theater.

In the center of Vermont, just five miles east of Rutland, is a flower of a country inn. (Wish I had said that but, in truth, it is on their brochure.) The red clover is the state flower of Vermont. The inn is the former summer home of General John Woodward.

This is a very comfortable inn. The rooms all have private baths. The living room has comfortable couches and chairs, and the tavern is a delightful spot to unwind in. Curl up in front of the fire with a good book and let the world whirl on by itself.

Owner-chef Dennis was tutored by his father and apprenticed in his kitchen in Switzerland. He is a fine chef. Dinner is served by candlelight. Fresh vegetables and fruit from their own and local farms are served here. ☛ Breakfast is not just a ho-hum thing. It is for real, with home-baked breads and muffins, omelets, and pancakes.

The view from the pool is beautiful. This is great country for hiking, biking and cross-country skiing or snowmobiling, or just resting.

How to get there: Take Route 4 east from Rutland, and the inn is on the right, down narrow Woodward Road.

♡

E: *Sundance is an inn horse. His friend is Four Square, recently retired from Skidmore College.*

*Even the riches of Kubla Khan cannot sway
the evenhanded hospitality of a proper innkeeper.*

Middlebury Inn
Middlebury, Vermont
05753

Innkeepers: Frank and Jane Emanuel
Telephone: 802-388-4961
Rooms: 80, 57 with private bath, 52 air-conditioned.
Rates: $30 and up, single; $34 to $56, double occupancy.
Facilities: Open all year. Breakfast, lunch, dinner, bar. Parking. Elevator, TV, skiing, bicyling.

There has been an inn standing at this same location since 1788. There have been some changes, due to fire and the inroads of time, but the original brick building was constructed in 1827. One hundred years later, when the Middlebury Hotel Company took over, a new heating plant was installed, and extensive repairs were made. The inn has a good central location, and of course, anyone who has anything to do with Middlebury College knows about the inn.

It is being managed now by Frank and Jane Emanuel and was recently awarded a restoration project grant by Vermont's Historic Preservation Division. There is a delightful veranda café, and a really large lobby. ☛ The dining room is beautiful, and the food that is served here is delicious. Upstairs the wide halls wander and dip, up one step and down three, wide enough for those ladies of long ago to have maneuvered their hoopskirts with grace.

How to get there: Go up Route 7, and you run right into Middlebury. The inn is in the middle of town.

E: *I could stay forever, mooning over the jigsaw puzzles in the lobby or eating their nightly popovers.*

Our sympathy for the hardships of our forbears should be somewhat mitigated by the fact that they had the best of country inns.

Zack's On The Rocks
Montgomery Center, Vermont
05471

Innkeepers: "Zack" and Gussie Zachadnyk (Zack)
Telephone: 802-326-4500
Rooms: One chalet, sleeps two.
Rates: $40 per night in summer; $50 in winter.
Facilities: Closed on Monday. Check during spring and fall for opening days. Bar, dinner only.

After you finally find Zack's you really will not believe what you see. His chalet, home and restaurant are literally hanging on the rocks over an incredible valley.

This is my smallest inn. A chalet that sleeps two has a living room, dining ell, kitchen, ☛ two fireplaces, a bedroom and a wow of a bathroom with a sunken tub. Even if you cannot stay here, stay in town and come up here to eat Zack's food. It is ☛ fantastic, and so are he and Gussie, his wife.

How to explain Zack's is almost impossible. When you approach the door of his restaurant you will find it is locked. Ring the sleigh bells, and the door will be opened by Zack. He will be in a wondrous costume and the performance begins. I will tell you no more except about the food. The menu is printed on a brown paper bag which is in beautiful contrast to his restaurant and Gussie's bar. Zack does all of the cooking. He is the most inventive chef and innkeeper I have had the pleasure to meet. The dining room has to be seen to be believed.

And Gussie's bar is something special. It has an organ with a full grand piano top built over it. This is my first organ bar. The room has a stone fireplace and is done pub style but with a flair. The bar has but five stools, but to go with it is the best stocked back-bar in Vermont. To top it all the inn plays music from the '40s. What a pleasant sound.

The inn dog is Gypsy, the largest German shepherd north of the Mason-Dixon line, and probably below as well. Pyewacket is a noisy Siamese cat who runs the inn and runs Zack.

Reservations here are an absolute must.

How to get there: Going north from Stowe on Route 100, turn left on Route 118 at Eden. When you reach Montgomery Center, turn right on Route 58. The inn is up the hill on the right, after the road becomes dirt.

E: *Zack's chalet is called Fore-the-Rocks. The private home is called Off-the-Rocks, and the inn is called On-the-Rocks. Gussie's bar is After-the-Rocks. Lots of rocks up here.*

olive Metcalf

Black Lantern Inn
Montgomery Village, Vermont
05470

Innkeepers: Rita & Allan Kalsmith
Telephone: 802-326-4507
Rooms: 11, all but two with private bath.
Rates: $26, EP.
Facilities: Closed first two weeks in May. Breakfast, dinner, bar, dining room. Parking. TV in lounge, skiing, fireplace.

When you get to Montgomery Village you are nearly in Canada, perhaps six or seven miles from the border. This is a quiet Vermont village, and the Black Lantern has been restored in the last year by its hard-working owners. Whether you come in the snow for a skiing vacation, or on a green summer day, there is a warm welcome at this friendly inn. It is also surprising to encounter a rather sophisticated menu in this out-of-the-way corner of the world.

You can ski at Jay Peak, where there are 50 miles of trails for every kind of skier, outright novice to expert. Not too far away, over the border, there are four Canadian mountains, and ski-week tickets are available. Cross-country skiing starts at the inn door, and is undoubtedly the best way to see beautiful Vermont in the winter.

Summer brings the joy of outdoor life. Fishing, swimming, golf, tennis, and hiking are all very near. You've heard about those country auctions, haven't you? Or would you rather spend the day browsing through antique shops? Whatever you choose to do, there will be a superbly quiet night to catch up on your sleep.

The double-peaked roof on this nice old, 1803, farmhouse covers a typical north-country inn. Small, friendly, and just a little bit different.

How to get there: Go north from Stowe on Route 100, and turn left on route 118 at Eden. This will take you into Montgomery Center. Continue down the main street and out of town, and before too long you will reach Montgomery Village and the inn. From I-89 in Burlington, turn right at St. Albans onto Route 105, toward Enosburg Falls. Pick up Route 118 at East Berkshire, and follow it into Montgomery Center. Follow the main street to Montgomery Village and the inn.

♎

E: *What is there that is so special about yellow cats? The youngster that greets you at the door is a charming feline.*

olive Metcalf

The Four Columns Inn
Newfane, Vermont
05345

Innkeeper: Jacques Alambert
Telephone: 802-365-7713
Rooms: 12, all with private bath, eight air-conditioned.
Rates: $45 to $60, EP, double occupancy.
Facilities: Closed in April, November, and on Mondays. Breakfast for house guests. Dinner from 6 to 9 p.m., jacket required. TV, bar. Parking. Dining room accessible to wheelchairs.

If the hearty goodness of your New England cooking should be starting to pall, turn your wheels toward The Four Columns Inn in Newfane. Here in an authentic New England village, in a lovely old house, you will find superb continental cuisine with a menu that will tease every palate.

Trout "au Bleu," plucked living from the inn's own tank, Curry Indonesian-Style, assorted hors d'oeuvres Parisienne, fresh Salmon Bernaise, rack of lamb for two, and many other delectable dishes are served.

Jacques Alambert is the new owner. He is from "Le

Bistro" in New York City, and he is inheriting the complete, fine staff of The Four Columns Inn.

Many of the rooms were made from the old barn that is connected, Vermont-style, to the house. Though the beams are rough, the freshness of the decor belies the house's age.

The wine list is excellent, as is to be expected, and it is also possible to obtain good American wine by the glass.

There is great swimming nearby, also wonderful skiing in winter. Newfane is a beautiful old town, and a few days spent here might not be the best thing for your figure, if you are not exercising, but when sublime food is at hand, who cares?

How to get there: The inn is 220 miles from New York, 100 miles from Boston. Take Exit 2 from I-91 at Brattleboro to Route 30 north. The inn is 100 yards off Route 30 on your left, in Newfane.

*I often wonder if a war could start
if the heads of confronting nations spent an evening
at a proper tavern.*

olive Metcalf

Old Newfane Inn
Newfane, Vermont
05345

Innkeepers: Eric and Gundy Weindl
Telephone: 802-365-4427
Rooms: 10, eight with private bath, two adjoining.
Rates: $46 to $60, per room, double occupancy.
Facilities: Closed April to mid-May, November 15 to December 15, and on Mondays. Continental breakfast included with room, lunch in summer, dinner year-round, bar. Parking.

Old is the right word to describe the Old Newfane Inn, founded in 1787, and carefully kept so that modern-day travellers can be cradled in its comfort.

It is nearly impossible to list the prizes won by the chef-owner, Eric Weindl. The food is outstandingly excellent. The rooms, few in number, are furnished with antiques, papered with quaint flowered wallpaper, and care has been taken to provide things like comfortable chairs and good reading lights.

☛ The dining room, with its beamed ceiling, is one of

the most attractive I have come upon in my travels. Eric and Gundy have been here for eight years and have become famous for the marvelous food they provide. World travellers, famous chefs, and food writers all make the trip up to Newfane, a gem of a town, with a well-deserved reputation as the garden spot of gastronomy.

How to get there: Take Exit 2 from I-91 in Brattleboro, and follow Route 30 north. The inn is on Route 30, on the left in Newfane.

Ė: How can I lose weight writing a country inn guide?

> *Come away, O human child!*
> *To the waters and the wild*
> *With a faery hand in hand . . .*
> William Butler Yeats

Olive Metcalf

Norwich Inn
Norwich, Vermont
05055

Innkeepers: Alden and Doreen Twachtman
Telephone: 802-649-1143
Rooms: 20, 18 with private bath.
Rates: $27 to $29 single, and $37 to $39 double, EP.
Facilities: Open all year. Breakfast, lunch, dinner, bar, cable
TV in all rooms, swimming nearby, skiing, canoeing,
and golf.

Right on the sign for the inn it says, "Since 1797," and it
is truly said, because travelers up the beautiful Connecticut
River Valley have been finding a warm welcome at this
grand old house ever since. Just a mile away from Dartmouth College, alumni, skiers, tourists and commercial
travelers find here a special homelike atmosphere that is
dignified but fun. A treat at hand is the ☛ Hopkins Center
in Hanover for music lovers.

You can come to Norwich by air, car, bus, or rail, or
walk if you must, but do come. Reserve well ahead during
football weekends, for this is the place to be. There is a great

room downstairs in the inn where the thick stone foundation of this old building is revealed, and it is here the losers and winners drown or celebrate their fortunes.

The food is very good, really exceptional. Rack of lamb or Norwich Inn Scallops are a treat, as is the duck à l'orange. The salad bar is one of the best I have found. Good also are the homemade breads. Lunch has a wide, good menu, but my favorites are the soup and salad combinations.

The big bow window in the dining room is a delight, but I think I like best to eat on the beautiful flower-filled porch, which is even used in the winter. You must see it in the snow.

With Hanover and Dartmouth right at hand you can find one good thing after another to do in this lovely area of Vermont and New Hampshire. In all seasons.

How to get there: Take Exit 13 from Route I-91. Go west a bit less than a mile to the center of town. The inn is on your left.

E: *A perfect drink spot is the dear little Victorian bar off the living room.*

Choose your inn, and enter in the world of relaxation.

olive Metcalf

Johnny Seesaw's
Peru, Vermont
05152

Innkeepers: Gary and Nancy Okun, and Jim and Margie Hessenthaler

Telephone: 802-824-5533

Rooms: 22, all with bath, plus ski bunk rooms for juniors.

Rates: $13 to $26 per room EPB, summer. $30 to $50 per person MAP, winter.

Facilities: Closed end of skiing to July 1, and end of foliage until Thanksgiving. Breakfast, dinner, picnic lunches extra, liquor license. Parking. TV, swimming, tennis, skiing, hunting.

The food at the inn is good, fine country food prepared with imagination, featuring home-baked bread and home-made soup. Val is the fine lady chef who turns out all this fine fare.

The inn has a unique character, mostly because of the guests who keep coming back. It is set 2,000 feet up, on Bromley Mountain. The 65 by 25-foot pool, marble rimmed, is a great summer gathering place, and the tennis court is always ready. There are six nearby golf courses, and riding is offered at the Ox Bow Ranch near Weston.

For the many skiers who come to Vermont, Bromley's five chairlifts and GLM Ski School are right next door. Stratton and Magic Mountains, the Viking Ski Touring Center, and Wild Wings X-C, are but a few minutes away.

For fishermen and hunters, or those who wish to take up the sport, the Orvis Fly-Fishing and Wing Shooting Schools in nearby Manchester have classes. The sportsman classes are held twice weekly, in three-day sessions through October, and participants may stay at the inn. The nearby towns boast many attractive and interesting shops.

How to get there: The inn is 220 miles from New York, 150 from Boston. From Route 7 take Route 30 right at Manchester Depot. The inn is 10 miles east, on Vermont Route 11. From I-91, follow Exit 6 to Route 103 to Chester. The inn is 20 miles west, on Vermont Route 11.

E: *The circular fireplace in the lounge really attracts me, to say nothing of the cushioned platform along one side of the room.*

The Wiley Foxx Inn
Peru, Vermont
05152

Innkeeper: Deborah Bixler
Telephone: 802-824-6600
Rooms: 18, nine with private bath.
Rates: $18 EPB summer; $30 to $36 MAP per person, double
occupancy.
Facilities: Open all year. Breakfast, dinner, BYOB bar. Fire-
places, game room, player piano, swimming pool, ski-
ing, hiking, and walking.

The inn is on Bromley Mountain in the Green Mountain National Forest. Located in the center of the golden
triangle comprised by Bromley, Magic, and Stratton Mountains, some of the best skiing in the East can be found here.
There is also a large variety of cross-country trails not far
from the inn.

For those who hike, there is the Long Trail, and also the
Appalachian Trail. Very near the inn you can find horseback
riding, canoeing, bicycling, or just plain, wonderful walking.
It is delightfully peaceful in this part of the mountains.

Rooms are cozy. Food is home cooked and hearty, with real country breakfasts and family-style dinners. ☛ Special are the homemade breads and desserts. The bar is BYOB, though the inn provides soda, ice, and soft drinks.

The game room is full of fun, with a player piano, games of every sort, magazines, and books, books, books. There is a plaque on the wall down here that particularly caught my fancy. It reads:

> *Oh how I wish I could foresee*
> *What is about to happen to me*
> *For here I am about to descend*
> *I pray the Lord I do not upend.*

The Skier's Prayer

How to get there: From I-91 take Exit 6, to Route 103, to Chester, Vermont. Go left onto Route 11, and the inn is approximately 20 miles beyond, in Peru.

E: *Five fireplaces in one inn. That is for me.*

Cats, birds, flowers, and dogs
in companionate confusion are to be found
where hospitality has bested the world of commerce.

The Golden Stage Inn
Proctorsville, Vermont
05153

Innkeepers: Tom & Wendy Schaaf
Telephone: 802-226-7744
Rooms: Ten, with private and semi-private baths.
Rates: In winter, $38, MAP, per person; in summer, $45, EPB per room, double occupancy. Ski packages available.
Facilities: Open year-round. Breakfast, dinner. Fireplaces, library, skiing, Steamtown trains, theater, golf, year-round tennis.

Here's an inn where you can bring your own horse, and the stables are elegant. Known locally still as The Skinner Place (that's Otis and his daughter Cornelia Otis Skinner, famed on the stage) this old house was once a stage stop, built shortly after Vermont's founding. Reputed to have been a stop on the "underground railroad," this house has had only six owners in its nearly 200 years. Tom and Wendy Schaaf have completely redecorated the inn, and Wendy has a marvelous garden here in summer.

☛ The food can only be described as delicious, hearty,

and traditionally New England. Dishes come side by side with continental cuisine like unusual quiches and superb veal. Wendy is the moving force behind the meals.

When winter comes there is skiing at nearby Okemo, Mount Ascutney, near I-91, or Round Top Mountain in Plymouth, with its special college rates and an excellent Junior Racing Program. At Killington there are year-round gondola rides, the longest in the country, and the seemingly longest snow season anywhere in the East.

On a summer day, or on one of those miraculously brilliant days in autumn, take a picnic and explore some of the acres of forests close to this cozy inn.

☛ Bike Vermont is another wonderful way to see this lovely country. While you bicycle to the next Vermont inn a support van comes around to transport your luggage. There are guides, and never more than 20 people in any group. Weekend and mid-week tours are offered from mid-May straight through the spectacular foliage season.

You are not very far from Weston, where there is a fine summer theater, and also the Inn at Weston, owned coincidentally, by Wendy's sister and brother-in-law.

How to get there: Take Route 103 north out of Chester, and just before you get to Ludlow you will see the Golden Stage on the right. From I-91, take Exit 8 onto Route 131 west to Proctorsville.

E: *Where to start? The garden, fantastic. The dogs, Okemo and Miss Piggy, and the cat named Twiggy don't know they are not supposed to be friends. It's all just lovely.*

olive Metcalf

Okemo Lantern Lodge
Proctorsville, Vermont
05153

Innkeepers: The Racicot Family
Telephone: 802-226-7770
Rooms: Seven, one with private bath.
Rates: $30 to $38 per person MAP.
Facilities: Open all year. Breakfast and dinner. Beer and wine
    license. All sports are nearby.

The first thing you notice when you enter the inn is a
monster of a spinning wheel in the front hall. In the living
room there is an exquisite old pump organ. This room is all
comfort, arm chairs, couches, a crackling fire to warm your
toes or, if you wish, stretch out on the chaise in a warm,
sunny bay window.

All of the guest rooms are attractive, and one has an
eyelet canopy bed.

Jan is "chief cook and bottle washer." The aroma of
🐖 fresh baked bread will wake you along with fresh
perked coffee and home-smoked bacon. If you have a special
occasion a 🐖 champagne breakfast in bed is a nice treat.

There is so much to do in this area year round. Spring is the time to watch the maple sugaring or just go fishing in one of the well stocked lakes or streams. In summer golf is nearby, so is tennis, hiking or bicycling. Fall is foliage and cider. Winter brings the skiing and skating, or you could also curl up with a good book by the fire.

How to get there: Take I-91 to Exit 6 in Bellows Falls. Go north on Route 103 to junction with Route 131, then left a quarter of a mile.

※

E: *Tumble in the Rumble, as it says in their brochure. In good weather a ride in the rumble seat of a 1935 Plymouth complete with a raccoon coat on the driver and assorted appropriate coats for the guests is my kind of fun.*

Spring flowers adding the final brush strokes at the edges of the granite walk to the inn's front stoop.

The Quechee Inn
Quechee, Vermont
05059

Innkeepers: Michael and Barbara Yaroschuk
Telephone: 802-295-3133
Rooms: 22, with private bath.
Rates: $48 to $70, double occupancy, EPB.
Facilities: Closed two weeks in April and early December. Breakfast and dinner, bar. Cross-country and downhill skiing, golf, tennis, swimming, boating, fishing, and hiking. Guest card to the Quechee Club.

The first time I saw and heard Quechee Gorge I was standing on the bridge that spans it. Now I know another way to see this remarkable quirk of nature. The inn is but one-half mile from it, and ☞ the innkeepers will show you how to see it from an unusual angle.

Quechee Inn was a private home from 1793 until 1976. Beautifully converted to an inn, it reflects the care the innkeepers give it. Some of the rooms have the largest ☞ four-poster, king-sized beds I have ever seen, others have twins, and all are equipped with cable color TV.

A brand new wing houses the kitchen and dining room, in addition to seven more guest rooms with picture windows overlooking the meadow and lake. Joining the dining room is a small library and conference room wired for audio-visual equipment. It's a real treat to be able to have a business meeting at a place like this. The living room has an abundance of comfortable couches and chairs, a piano, color TV, books, and a fireplace. One feels at home here any season of the year.

The inn guests have full club privileges at the Quechee Club. The golf courses are breathtakingly scenic and are great tests of golf. If you do intend to play, let the inn know when you call for reservations so they can arrange a tee off time for you.

A new addition to this lovely spot is a golden retriever named Governor Marsh.

How to get there: From I-91 take Route 89 north to Exit 1. Go west on Route 4 for 1.2 miles, then right on Club House Road for one mile to the inn.

E: *Old-fashioned New England dining with homemade breads,* sticky buns, *and regional specials such as trout and venison make a visit here a must.*

Saxtons River Inn
Saxtons River, Vermont
05154

Innkeepers: Averill Campbell Larsen and The Campbell Family
Telephone: 802-869-2110
Rooms: 11, with private baths.
Rates: $20 single; $25 to $45, double occupancy, continental breakfast included.
Facilities: Closed in January. Restaurant is open Thursday, Friday, Saturday, and Sunday in February and March. Breakfast for house guests, lunch, dinner, bar. Parking.

Blessings on the Campbell family, and especially on Averill Campbell, who has brought everyone home from the four corners of the earth to renovate this turn-of-the-century inn and revitalize the little village of Saxtons River. ☛ Cross the wide front porch and come through the gracious front door. To the right is a little breakfast room, to the left, the copper bar. Straight ahead is the dining room. Tiffany chandeliers light the flower-bedecked tables, and some of the freshest, most original food is brought out from the spick-and-span kitchen to please even the most particular diner.

☞ The guest rooms are spectacular, handsomely decorated with a combination of old furniture and crisp new fabrics. Your innkeeper has travelled around the world and knows what is needed for creature comforts, including pleasant places to read, with lights in the right places. She has slept in every one of her guest rooms, an acid test, and she has her own aerie at the top of the tower, five stories above the world of Saxtons River.

The menu changes, of course, with what is fresh and good in season. If you are really not hungry you can have soup and salad for a most nominal price. If you are starving, begin with soup or mushroom maison, rumaki or ratatouille, and go on to a main course of steak, Chicken Louise, or Cocquille St. Jacques. But be sure to save room for dessert. They are appallingly good, and are outlawed by every diet-club in the country.

How to get there: Take either Exit 5 or 6, at Bellows Falls, from I-91. Pick up Route 5, and proceed to Route 121. Saxtons River is on Route 121, and the inn is on Main Street in the center of town.

E: *I love to read in bed, and this is the most comfortable place for doing it.*

olive Metcalf

The Fundador Lodge
South Londonderry, Vermont
05155

Innkeeper: Mort Marton
Telephone: 802-297-1700
Rooms: 16 with bath, three bunkrooms, each with bath.
Rates: Winter $94 to $98, double occupancy MAP; summer $44 to $48, double occupancy EP. Slightly higher weekends.
Facilities: Closed mid-April to June 1, and October 27 until Thanksgiving. Breakfast, dinner, bar, swimming pool, two Har-Tru tennis courts with club house, skiing with cross-country on the property.

There is no end to the things you can do right at this inn and close by. For skiers you are minutes from Bromley, Stratton and Magic mountains. But skiers or not, Mort, in his quiet way, makes sure all the guests are happy. In ski season he gives a breakfast report on the snow conditions from every nearby slope and even cuts ☞ a wedge of snow, brings it in and proves to all how the skiing will be. ☞ Those who are left behind are offered trips to nearby areas for education, and really mostly for fun.

The main lounge is huge, with a circular fireplace, a Steinway concert grand (for all to play), great couches and card tables. Rooms here are very comfortable and modern. There is also a library loaded with books.

The Peppermill Restaurant derives its name from Mort's past accomplishments in the design field. Here are ☛ all the mills, a great spice rack and even a ☛ cork ice bucket that won a silver medal for the United States and Mort at the Triennial di-Milano.

The food is gourmet and is an art form all in itself. Mushrooms stuffed with snails and ☛ a ton of garlic, boneless smoked trout, chicken piccata, and jumbo shrimp scampi are but a few of the delightful delicacies. As for desserts, try the freshly-baked meringues with blueberries and fresh whipped cream. Dickinsons' jellies and jams are served here with just marvelous breakfasts. Do try branola toast or cinnamon pancakes. And the dining room is warmly done in cozy shades of blue.

The bar and lounge areas are just what you would expect, perfect, with bumper pool that I love.

How to get there: Take Exit 2 (Brattleboro) off I-91. Follow Route 30 north to South Londonderry (Rawsonville). The inn is on your left just beyond where Route 100 turns north.

E: *Three collies—Fyfie, Chumley and Kiwy—really run the inn.*

Olive Metcalf

The Londonderry Inn
South Londonderry, Vermont
05155

Innkeeper: James Bushby
Telephone: 802-824-5226
Rooms: 26, 23 with private bath, five family rooms.
Rates: $32 to $50, EP, double occupancy. Special ski packages.
Facilities: Closed mid-October to December, and April to June 1. Bar, breakfast, lunch in summer, dinner. Billiard room, skiing, swimming pool, paddle tennis, buggy rides, sleigh rides, special cross-country trails. Two ground floor rooms, and restaurant accessible to wheelchairs.

High on a hill overlooking the village of South Londonderry sits this exciting four-season inn, central to three big ski areas, Bromley, Magic Mountain, and Stratton.

Summer gives you a large, heated swimming pool, horseback riding, and great hiking and biking trails. Around the year there is indoor recreation with a great, vintage billiard table, Ping-Pong, and many comfortable places to relax, read a book, needlepoint, or just stare at the huge blazing fireplace.

The food here is outstanding. The meals are served buffet-style in the beautifully decorated old dining room, which used to be the woodshed for the inn and was built in 1826. The emphasis is on ☛ home-cooked, country-style foods, with the one meal served each night often accompanied by specials. The entrees include prime rib of beef, roast turkey, roast ham, roast lamb, a complete New England boiled dinner, and on every Friday, fresh fish. Meals feature delicious homemade soups, and ice creams with hot fudge or butterscotch sauce, and homemade pies. The price is reasonable, and of interest to hungry skiers and hikers, you get all you can eat. In the summertime the inn serves a sumptuous and renowned Sunday brunch.

The inn has an extensive wine list, but of particular interest are the special selections designed to accompany the meal of the evening. All of these wines are moderately priced and come from many different vineyards in California.

The rooms are neat, clean, and comfortable, and all have ☛ down pillows and ☛ large, thirsty towels. These things are far too often overlooked by innkeepers.

How to get there: Take Exit 1 or 2 from I-91 at Brattleboro, and follow Route 30 north to Rawsonville. Then take Route 100 to South Londonderry. The inn is on Main Street.

E: *The special events here are cookouts by the pool, and from time to time, genuine New England clambakes.*

Charda
Stowe, Vermont
05672

Innkeepers: Julius and Trudy Tarlo
Telephone: 802-253-4598
Rooms: 11, all with private bath.
Rates: Summer $20, winter $32 EPB, double occupancy.
Facilities: Closed between Thanksgiving and Christmas, and
from mid-April to Memorial Day. Breakfast for house
guests, dinner, bar, ramps available for wheelchairs in
the dining room.

Charda looks as though it belongs in the Alps, though it comes complete with the charm and food of a fine Hungarian restaurant. The inn has a splendid view of Mount Mansfield and Spruce Peak. ☛ The old barn was turned into rooms, and believe me, the Tarlo's have done a fine job. Some rooms have a double bed and a twin, and all have private baths for a very comfortable stay.

☛ Hungarian food at its best is served here, featuring favorites like stuffed cabbage, Kasseler Rippchen, smoked loin of pork with sauerkraut, Hungarian beef goulash, and

Wiener Bachendle, which is a boneless breast of chicken prepared like a schnitzel with rice and mushrooms. The desserts, to name but a few, include ☛ chestnut puree topped with whipped cream, Kahlua and chocolate sprinkles; cheesecake with black cherries in a rum topping; and more, if you forget your diet.

The small bar in the center of this lovely dining room has an ☛ espresso and cappuccino machine that turns out heavenly coffees. Converted oil lamps hang from the ceiling of the dining room and from the windows, which have stained glass in them. Just look out at the magnificent mountain range. The wine list is unusual, with many selections from Hungary, Austria and Germany. And, of course, there are good imported beers.

One more note on desserts: they have Palacsinta. You must go and find out about this one for yourself.

How to get there: Take Route I-89 off I-91, to Route 100, and go north. The inn is on the left, north of Stowe.

E: *The inn cat is a beauty of a calico named Malisa.*

Inn keeping takes twenty-five hours
of every twenty-four, but done right
it makes a wonderful life.

Edson Hill Manor
Stowe, Vermont
05672

Innkeeper: Laurence P. Heath; John and Joann Rybak, managers.

Telephone: 802-253-7371

Rooms: 11, seven baths in the manor, six rooms and three baths in the annex. Some suites. Fireplaces in some bedrooms.

Rates: $45 to $65 per person, MAP.

Facilities: Closed in November, and May to mid-June. Breakfast, lunch, dinner. Parking. Apres-ski lounge, stables, ski shop, golf at Stowe Country Club, pool, ice skating in Stowe, stocked trout pond, pitch-n'-putt golf.

Here you are, halfway between Stowe and Mount Mansfield, 1500 feet above the hubble-bubble of that lively village of Stowe that is growing every year. Here is truly luxurious living, in a house that was built in 1939 for a family that loved to ski and ride.

☛ The swimming pool here is beautiful. It won an award from Paddock Pools of California. The stocked trout pond is a must for anglers. When the snow comes, ☛ the stables turn into a cross-country ski center, so there you are, practically taking off from the inn door.

This attractive house has been run as an inn since 1953, and there are still homelike touches. The pine paneled living room has an aura of quiet elegance that reflects the feeling of gracious living all too often missing from our busy lives.

There are so many different rates and packages for so many different activities, I suggest you write for the complete set of brochures.

How to get there: Take Route 108 north from Stowe, 4.9 miles, turn right on Edson Hill Road, and follow the signs, uphill, to the Manor.

E: *The old Delft tiles around many of the fireplaces are so appealing. Look closely at the living room curtains. Somebody shopped hard for that material.*

The cheers of millions are for politicians,
while the quiet appreciation of a well cooked chop
is but for a few.

Foxfire Inn
Stowe, Vermont
05672

Innkeepers: Irene and Art Segreto
Telephone: 802-253-8459
Rooms: Five, plus chalets, all with bath.
Rates: In summer, $15 to $18, EP, per person; in winter, $28
to $32, MAP, double occupancy.
Facilities: Open all year. Breakfast, dinner, bar. Parking.
Swimming, skiing.

The Segretos want to welcome old and new friends, and
there are myriads of them, to their inn. The house is over 150
years old and has been restored to easy comfort by these
enthusiastic innkeepers. And there is so much to do here,
from the finest skiing in the East to great lounging by the
pool.

There is a beautiful inn dog, Coby, a "formerly white"
Samoyed who smiles his secret smile to greet you. Irene says
he is just impossible to keep clean, but he did not look that
dingy to me. Could be the contrast with the snow.

Irene has created a 🐾 garden room that is a great spot

202

for lunch. It is all white lattice with loads of hanging plants. This is a gazebo to end them all.

The best Italian kitchen in New England may seem a bit misplaced so far north in Vermont, but it is here. Taste, and you will agree. The ☛ tomato sauce is an old family recipe brought over from Naples. And do try things like baked broccoli, which is a combination of tomato sauce, ricotta cheese, and broccoli. There are seven different and delicious veal dishes. Boneless breast of chicken is prepared five ways, and the Eggplant Parmigiana has a special place in my heart. Shrimp Marinara I can still taste. As the front of the menu says, here you discover "The Italian Art of Eating."

And when you can push yourself away from the table, you have Stowe at your door, with antiques, shops, skiing, skating, walking, hiking, fishing, and more.

How to get there: Take I-89 to Route 100 north into Stowe. The inn is on the right, north of town.

☙

E: *Pass me another tortoni, please. I am settled in for the season.*

A cricket on the hearth of a country inn
is music beyond the angels.

Spruce Pond Inn
Stowe, Vermont
05672

Innkeepers: Max and Margaret Holland
Telephone: 802-253-4828
Rooms: 18, 14 with private bath.
Rates: $28 to $45, EP, double occupancy.
Facilities: Closed from Easter to May 15, and October 15 to
    December 1. Breakfast, dinner, bar, air-conditioning.

The first thing you see when you enter the inn is a black bear coat rack with three cubs from the Black Forest in Germany. A stroll down the brick walkway, full of plants, you pass by a very unusual grandfather's clock, oriental in style. In ☞ 1740 it went from England to China for its beautiful engraving, then shipped back to England, and now it lives here.

The bar-lounge is a wonderful place to unwind after skiing, hiking, biking or whatever you do. It is a very comfortable bar with chairs, couches and a large stone fireplace. The living room also has a huge fireplace with generous couches and chairs. All in all, wherever you decide to relax, you will find a place to put it.

Food here is excellent. The menu is expansive. A few of the goodies are broiled king-crab legs, chicken Chasseur and veal Oscar. Another treat are their flambe dishes cooked at your table. A fine wine cellar makes it all go together.

Stowe is a skier's paradise, Mount Mansfield and Spruce Peak offer the best skiing in the east. Cross-country buffs have miles of trails. Others can enjoy tobogganing, skating and country sleigh rides.

For children "The Old Milk House" is a delightful recreation spot. It is adjacent to the inn and has games for the whole family.

How to get there: Take I-89 to Route 100 north. The inn is on the left going into town.

🌹

E: *A swim in the spring-fed pond is for the brave, but between shivers the view is superb.*

*A country inn piled high with snow
is a cheery fortress against the cold.*

olive Metcalf

Echo Lake Inn
Tyson, Vermont
05149

Innkeepers: Mark and Jo Brown
Telephone: 802-228-8602
Rooms: 23, six with private bath.
Rates: $29 to $42 MAP, per person.
Facilities: Closed first two weeks in April. Breakfast, lunch in fall and summer. Dinner, bar, TV lounge, heated pool, tennis, golf, fishing, skiing, boating, bicycles and horseback riding.

Echo Lake is an authentic "old colonial inn" that has been welcoming travelers for 175 years. The inn has been completely restored and modernized, including ☞ an automatic fire alarm system, but its charm has been retained; hence their slogan, "The charm of old Vermont."

For your comfort you may relax in one of the exquisitely appointed bedrooms, all of which have been recently redecorated. The new dormitories are perfect for large skiing or hiking groups, or great for a family.

The dining room is watched over by a young chef just

206

out of the five-year training program at the Woodstock Inn. He serves marvelous food, or as our innkeeper says, "Boy can he cook." From fish, fresh daily, to the chef's specials, which range from chicken, roasts, steaks and chops, there is something for everyone here; and it always can be topped off with the homemade fruit pies that are made daily.

For your enjoyment the inn's living room, with a cheery fireplace, is perfect for a game of cards, reading, or just relaxing. There is a large, heated swimming pool with a bathhouse and shower facilities. And the sandy beach on Echo Lake is but 100 yards from the inn. ☞ The inn has rowboats, canoes, and sailboats for you to enjoy. Echo is the middle lake of the three-stream, spring-fed Plymouth Lakes.

A nice touch at the inn are the all-weather tennis courts, lighted for night play. And for you winter buffs the skiing season is long up here in northern Vermont, and there are six good alpine areas nearby.

How to get there: Take Exit 6 from I-91. Turn right on Route 100 in Ludlow. The inn is on your left in Tyson before you get to Plymouth Union.

☾

E: *The lakes mirror the brilliant colors of fall like nowhere else in New England. Spectacular!*

Tucker Hill Lodge
Waitsfield, Vermont
05673

Innkeepers: Carter Parkinson, owner; Emily & Zeke Church, managers.
Telephone: 802-496-3983
Rooms: 20, 11 with private baths, others share.
Rates: $26 to $38, MAP, per person.
Facilities: Open all year. No food off season. Breakfast for house guests, dinner, bar. Skiing, tennis, swimming pool, cross-country lunches, Sunday brunch only through October.

You will find Tucker Hill Lodge nestled on a wooded ridge overlooking the road that winds up to the Mad River Glen Ski Area. ☛ Route 17, by the way, is one of the most spectacular roads you will ever find.

The inn is cozy, ☛ fresh flowers in your room, hand-made quilts on most of the beds, comfortable living rooms and caring innkeepers.

The menu changes every day, and the food is excellent, with inventive dishes like shrimp and watercress salad with a vinaigrette gourmande dressing or avocado and grapefruit salad with a dressing of grapefruit and lemon juice, scallions and olive oil. The veal is tender and light. One way it is served is with asparagus sauce, another is with lemon sabayon sauce. I like the different touches the chef has up here. They also serve interesting fish dishes like poached tile fish with shrimp and leeks or poached monk fish with a tomato beurre blanc sauce. Of course beef and chicken are on the menu too. And would you believe a coffee called Dastardly Mash? Come on up and try it.

There is a lot doing up here, tennis, skiing, of course, and a Robert Trent Jones golf course nearby. There is plenty of fishing or just relax in this lovely inn. Do remember to pet Blue, the inn dog.

How to get there: Turn off Route 100 onto Route 17. This is the Mad River Valley.

E: *I cannot think of a nicer place to sit than on the deck, under the trees, sipping something long and cool, or I'll take the menu, one item at a time, from Tabouli, Seviche, to roast pork with mustard sauce. Yum, yum.*

To find a good inn as darkness glowers on the horizon, there is no treasure to match it.

Olive Metcalf

Acorn Lodge
Waterbury Center, Vermont
05677

Innkeepers: Beverly & George Ostler
Telephone: 802-244-5543
Rooms: Five, some with bath.
Rates: $30 to $40, double occupancy. Country breakfast included.
Facilities: Closed from November to Christmas week, and in April. Breakfast for house guests, dinner served Saturday night by reservation, no bar, BYOB. Parking. Swimming, skiing, cooking school by reservation in June, July, and August, and September. Bedroom accessible to wheelchairs.

Nestled in a rolling valley just a few minutes south of Stowe, the Acorn Lodge is close to everything that is happening in northern Vermont. Sit in the fabulous conversation pit by the fire when you come home from the slopes. The double-faced fireplace that divides the conversation pit from the dining room is divine. The beer can collection is unique, and the chess and backgammon boards make this a top place to relax.

The inn is a restored farmhouse built in 1835. You will find year-round antiquing, and in summer, fishing and hiking by babbling Vermont streams. Fall brings the crisp foliage, and winter, of course, covers the slopes with snow. Comfortable rooms and the country dining room add much charm.

Every cook of every persuasion who walks in will be mad about the kitchen, with its circular island under the old chandelier that holds all the pots. June, July, and August are by reservation only at the Acorn, as Beverly runs a vacation cooking school. This is my idea of the perfect way to vacation while you learn about good food.

There is a spring-fed pond on the property for great summer swimming and good winter skating. The garden and the house plants are lush. The pure spring water must be the reason.

How to get there: South of Stowe, on Route 100, turn onto Gregg Hill Road. This is four miles north of I-89, between Burlington and Montpelier.

E: Talk about cooking! School never tasted better.

The Inn at Weathersfield
Weathersfield, Vermont
05151

Innkeepers: Mary Louise and Ron Thorburn
Telephone: 802-263-9217
Rooms: Five, one suite, all with private bath.
Rates: $45 to $55 per room EPB.
Facilities: Closed mud season and end of November. Breakfast, lunch July 4th through October and by advance reservations in winter. Dinner Wednesday through Saturday. High tea. Service bar, large library, horse and carriage stalls.

This beautiful old inn was built circa 1776 and has a wonderful history. At one point in the Civil War it was an important stop on the "underground railroad" hiding slaves en route to Canada. The inn is set well back from the road. Your rest is assured.

The rooms are beautiful, with ☛ fresh flowers, fresh fruit, canopy beds, electric sheets, ☛ feathered pillows, stencilled walls. At night your bed is turned down and a candy placed on your pillow.

☞ Breakfast, complete with fresh squeezed orange juice, is served in your room. The dining room, once the carriage house, has a good part of its walls lined with books, and above the books a fascinating bottle collection. The innkeepers are both accomplished musicians and can be persuaded to play. Ron played the piano for me while I had lunch. He has a nice touch on the keys. The food is imaginative and different. ☞ Cider jelly is made nearby and used in some cooking. I never had had it before, so I bought some and used it as a baste on lamb chops at home. Delicious! Chicken Weathersfield is just one of Mary Louise's recipes that does wonderful things with boneless breast of chicken.

The inn has many mulberry trees from which the owners make a sweet and sour mulberry sauce, one use for which is on stuffed pork chops. The beautiful silver serving pieces are functional as well as decorative. To make all things work just right, Ron has an ☞ extensive and good wine cellar.

Daughter Heather and husband, Jack, are potters. Their fine work is used in the inn, and certain pieces are for sale here.

How to get there: Exit 7 from I-91. Take Route 11 to Springfield, Vermont and then Route 106 north to Perkinsville. About one-half mile short of the village you will find the inn on your left set well back from the road.

E: *A wassail cup is served from a cauldron in the keeping room fireplace. High tea is a special I love along with a gaggle of inn dogs known as "Mom's Moldy Muppets."*

Grandmother's House
West Arlington, Vermont
05250

Innkeeper: Mrs. Walter Finney
Telephone: 802-375-2328
Rooms: Five, with 2½ baths.
Rates: $25 per person overnight, with two meals, $40. Reservations and deposit required. Mrs. Finney really likes you to stay at least two nights.
Facilities: Open all year. Breakfast and dinner, no bar. Parking. Fishing, tennis, croquet, horseshoes.

Of course, you must go over the river and through the covered bridge to reach Grandmother's House. When you arrive, you may find a hand-lettered sign on the door saying, "Grandmother Washing Hair. Holler loudly." Mrs. Finney, official Grandmother to the world, has a whole file of signs for any occasion. She prefers her guests to stay more than one night. If you stay awhile, you can really begin to relax.

☛ This is a superb place for fishermen. Don't ask about antique shops, Mrs. Finney doesn't go to them. Her house is filled with beautiful things, and one of her prizes is a tiger maple four-poster, made by her (we think) great, great grandfather.

Loaf under the great shady maples, play tennis, croquet or horseshoes, take long walks along country lanes, or ski in winter. Once upon a time Norman Rockwell, the artist, lived in this house, and you are right across the lane from a dear little Methodist church.

How to get there: Turn off Route 7 in Arlington, onto Route 313. Go about five miles to a covered bridge on the left, and cross that bridge to Grandmother's House.

E: *Look at the figures holding the plants on each side of the porch. They came from Mrs. Finney's grandmother's conservatory. They are charming.*

I have enjoyed the hospitality of a good inn and I am ready for the day ahead.

The Inn at Sawmill Farm
West Dover, Vermont
05356

Innkeepers: Rodney and Ione Williams
Telephone: 802-464-8131
Rooms: 20, all with private bath.
Rates: In season $100 to $160, MAP double occupancy; off
  season $90 to $140.
Facilities: Closed last day of November to December 12.
  Breakfast for house guests, dinner, bar, swimming pool,
  tennis, 2½-acre trout fishing pond. No credit cards.

Rod and Ione Williams have transformed an old Vermont barn into the gayest, warmest, most attractive inn that
I have seen in many a country mile. Ione is a professional
decorator and Rod is an architect, which makes for a wonderful marriage of talents for a just perfect inn, indoors and
out.

Gardens greet you as you drive up, and once inside you
will find lots of barn siding cleverly used with interesting
antique farm implements hung thereon. The copper collection around the ☛ oversized fireplace is a sight to see, and

the huge copper-topped coffee table nearby is a beauty. The 🖙 library is an old hayloft over the end of the living room, and a majestic place for the solitary reader.

The Pot Belly Lounge has an 🖙 incredible bar of solid copper. It also houses the Williams' collection of ancient ice skates, biscuit tins, and a player piano that really works. Beyond the bar is an enclosed porch that contains a small greenhouse. When I was there this spring it was full of passion flowers and bouganvillea, and is a very nice spot to enjoy the wonderful food that is served.

The Williams' son, Brill, runs the kitchen. Ione does the pies. Both are fussy and excellent cooks. What a nice family combination for the inn business.

Accommodations are very different, with some Victorian rooms, some done in Chippendale, and all with the flavor of New England at its best. A few suites have fireplaces, and my favorite is the Cider House. All are color-coordinated with 🖙 thick towels and extra pillows. And as a final touch 🖙 fresh fruit is served in your room.

How to get there: Take Route I-91 to Brattleboro. Take Exit 9 west to Wilmington, and then follow Route 100 about five miles to West Dover.

E: The inn makes a special of special times. Do try to get up here for Christmas. It's something you will never forget.

Olive Metcalf

Snow Den Inn
West Dover, Vermont
05356

Innkeepers: Milt and Jean Cummings
Telephone: 802-464-9355
Rooms: Nine, eight with private baths.
Rates: $30 to $40 per room EP. Write for package rates.
Facilities: Closed April and May. Breakfast, lunch in summer.
   Dinner in winter. BYOB. All summer and winter sports
   nearby.

   Snow Den is a nice name for an inn up here in snow
country. There is so much to keep you busy and happy in this
area. The inn is two miles from Mt. Snow and two minutes
from the Mt. Snow Golf Course. Skiing, snowmobiling,
cross-country skiing and all sorts of other season activities
are at hand.
   The inn is informal and comfortable. The den is large,
has a picture window that overlooks Mt. Snow and has a
fireplace. A good place to relax after a day's activities. The
bedrooms are large. ☛ One is done in my favorite color,
blue.

Milt is the chef. One entree is served each night. Some friends reported that breakfast was yummy, french toast, eggs, crisp bacon and homemade zucchini nut bread.

And to make things warm and wonderful, there is a nice wood stove in the dining room.

How to get there: Take Route I-91 to Brattleboro. Take Route 9 west to Wilmington, and then follow Route 100 about five miles to West Dover. The inn is on your right in the middle of the village.

E: *The inn was built in 1885 and was the first ski lodge at Mt. Snow.*

> *"Does the road wind uphill all the way?*
> *Yes, to the very end.*
> *Will the day's journey take the whole day long?*
> *From morn to night, my friend."*
> Christina Rossetti

Olive Metcalf

The Weathervane Lodge
West Dover, Vermont
05356

Innkeepers: Liz and Ernie Chabot
Telephone: 802-464-5426
Rooms: Ten, four with private bath, plus two apartments.
Rates: $13 to $23 per person EP, $26 to $34 MAP.
Facilities: Never closed. Breakfast, dinner only in winter.
   BYOB bar, lounge, two large suites with kitchen and
   fireplace.

When I drove in the parking lot of the Weathervane I
met the inn cat, Spooky, sleeping under a car. Cesar, the
loveable shepherd, gave a small woof.
   This is a family inn that ☛ never closes. It is warmly
furnished with authentic antiques and has tons of colonial
charm. One of the suites might suit your family rather well.
It has two bedrooms, a kitchen and a living room with a
fireplace.
   Dinner is served in the winter only, and breakfast in
both winter and summer. There are a variety of restaurants
in the area to choose from in the off seasons.

The lounge and recreation room have a set-up bar where you bring your own bottle, enjoy the fireplace, piano, play Ping-Pong and have fun.

There is much to do here all seasons, but do remember that this is a family inn, not as fancy as some, but a good place for a relaxing few days.

How to get there: From Wilmington take Route 100 north to West Dover. The inn is on the Dorr Fitch Road.

E: *I like keeping things in the family, especially as in this case, when it was the inn. The son of this inn's family married the daughter of the Keepers of On The Rocks Inn.*

*For one night at least
let me escape from all those things
the Puritans tell me I must face.
Let me find a friendly inn.*

221

West Dover Inn
West Dover, Vermont
05356

Innkeepers: Alice O'Toole, Walter and Joan Rosenthal
Telephone: 802-464-5207
Rooms: 19, two with private baths.
Rates: $26 to $35, double occupancy EP.
Facilities: Closed end of April for a few days. Breakfast and dinner. Full service bar. TV in sitting room.

This old inn was in my book once before when Chet Hagedorn owned it. Now it has new owners, and I thought it should return to the guide, mainly because I do believe we need inns for all sorts of people. This is a perfect inn for visits by full families. It is a warm, nice inn, not fancy, but good.

The food served here is good. The inn special is ☞ baked seafood supreme; clams, shrimp and crabmeat baked with real cream and topped with parmesan cheese. Yum, yum. There is also a fresh spinach salad, good soups and lots more to go with the special of the day.

There are a wealth of things to do in this area of Vermont every season of the year. For winter you have skiing, both cross-country and alpine. For the warmer months you have golf, tennis, horseback riding, hiking and walking. Boats and canoes are on Lake Whitingham which is 12 miles away. Nearby lakes provide swimming. Vermont is beautiful to see and to play in, so come and enjoy.

How to get there: Take Exit 2 from I-91 at Brattleboro, Vermont, then take Route 9 west to Route 100 north. In West Dover you will find the inn on your right in the village.

E: *The magnificent old piano in the parlor is a dream.*

Let us escape for a day, or better a week,
and hide away in a country inn.

olive Metcalf

Windham Hill Farm
West Townshend, Vermont
05359

Innkeepers: Betty and Jim Seagers
Telephone: 802-874-4080
Rooms: 10, most with private bath. Capacity of 26, with bunk
rooms for youngsters or skiers.
Rates: $40 to $45, MAP, double occupancy.
Facilities: Closed after foliage until snow falls, and at the end
of snow season to May 15. Breakfast and dinner, no bar,
BYOB. Complimentary wine served with dinner.

At Windham Hill Farm you are sitting on the top of the
world looking down on creation. ☞ The West River Valley
stretches as far as the eye can see. Except for a small farmhouse on a neighboring hilltop, there is no sign of man's
unkindly hand. This 135-year-old farmhouse has been carefully restored.

The family-style meals here are memorable. Betty
makes all the breads and desserts in her own kitchen, and
Jim whips up a storm of appetizers, soups, and entrees that
are sure to tease your palate. In season all ☞ the vegetables

are fresh, many of them grown right on the farm. There is a fresh water pond used for wading in summer, skating in winter, and a new terrace building that overlooks it all. Indoors, there are books, music, piano, games, TV, old magazines, fireplaces, and the lounge.

There are plants, a stack of period *Life* magazines and a well-stocked library, with everything from Barbara Cartland to Aldous Huxley. The rooms—many with their own porch verandas—have names, not numbers. There is no bar as such, but complimentary wine is served with dinner, and you are welcome to bring your own cocktails.

If you are looking for one of the more remote, exquisite, peaceful, and captivating places to unwind, forget your cares, and utterly relax in an unorganized way, come to Windham Hill Farm.

How to get there: North from Greenfield on I-91, take the second Brattleboro exit, marked West Brattleboro and Vermont 9. Then go east on Vermont 9 to Brattleboro's Main Street. Go north three blocks to the Exxon station, bear left on Vermont Route 30 to West Townshend for 21 miles. At the Country Store, turn right, up the hill, on Windham Road. You are 1½ miles from the Windham Hill Farm sign, which is on the right.

E: The new wing also has a new dining room overlooking the frog pond.

olive Metcalf

The Inn at Weston
Weston, Vermont
05161

Innkeepers: Stu & Sue Douglas
Telephone: 802-824-5804
Rooms: 13, 10 with bath.
Rates: $39 to $42 per person, MAP.
Facilities: Closed November, and mid-April to mid-May. Dining room closed Wednesday. Breakfast, dinner, Sunday brunch, bar. TV, fireplaces in lounge and pub. Wheelchair ramp available for dining room and one ground floor bedroom.

If you walk in the front door of this lovely inn, you are in Sue Douglas' kitchen, and Sue is the chef. She greets you with a warm smile and great culinary treats. The weekend I was here, the fare was 🐄 poached salmon with mustard sauce, roast beef, Chicken Kiev, and a Greek dinner salad. There is a different dinner salad served each night.

Stu is the breakfast chef, and he makes marvelous 🐄 whole wheat, cornmeal and rye pancakes, or French toast made from Sue's homemade breads. It is all served with

Vermont bacon and maple syrup. The homemade apple butter contains whole slices of apple, and the blueberry muffins are so good.

The rooms are small, very very pleasant with old antique beds that are comfortable. The dining room has so much charm and warmth, with walls of real barn siding, and everyone who works here smiles. They are a happy group.

Weston is the home of the Vermont Country Store. It is a short stroll down the road, and a mecca for browsers. The inn is close to several ski areas, so do come and enjoy. As the Douglases say, "This is where friendships begin," and they really do. If you are on a special diet, tell Sue and she will try to help you stay within it.

How to get there: Off I-91, on Exit 6, take Route 103 to Chester. Follow Route 11 to Londonderry, and turn right on Route 100 to Weston. The inn is in the Village.

E: *Afternoon tea is served at 4, with hot spiced cider and Sue's homemade goodies—Wow!*

> To eat merely to live
> is a crime against man
> for which the gibbet is
> inadequate punishment.

Brook Bound
Wilmington, Vermont
05363

Innkeepers: The Fajans
Telephone: 802-464-5267
Rooms: Nine, five with private bath, two housekeeping chalets.
Rates: $23 to $30 per person.
Facilities: Closed mid-October to mid-December, and mid-April to mid-June. Breakfast, dinner, swimming pool, recreation room, pool table, Ping-Pong, tennis.

"In the beautiful Green Mountains of southern Vermont, off a country road in a lovely quiet setting with commanding views of Haystack and Mount Snow, there is this warm and friendly inn waiting to welcome you." This is a quote from the inn's brochure, and it is so well said.

The grounds are spacious, and the ☞ pool is heated. It sits up above the inn with the tennis courts beyond. There are glorious big trees all over, and in the fall they are a sight to behold.

Food here is served family-style, with much of it home-grown. Set-ups are provided for your drink, and in the winter it all happens around a neat fireplace. The inn has ☞ a refrigerator especially for guests to keep luncheon food and snacks or drinks. We think this is a nice thing to do.

Two chalets are close by. The smaller one holds up to six people and the larger one can accommodate 11. You do your own cooking and housekeeping.

The inn is close to several ski areas for both downhill and cross-country. There is so much to do up in this area any season of the year that it would take pages just to list everything.

You are only 12 miles from the Marlboro Music Festival or the Brattleboro Music Center's Bach program. A real turn-on for a music lover.

How to get there: From Wilmington take Route 100 north and turn left on Cold Brook Road. Go 2.3 miles to the inn.

E: *Animals again. Heather is a lovely collie and there is a cat, a cat by the name of Fuzzy. They also breed, train, and board Morgan horses.*

A warming fire, a strong drink, a genial innkeeper . . .
and winter is somewhere in the hills but is not here.

Olive Metcalf

The Hermitage
Wilmington, Vermont
05363

Innkeeper: James McGovern
Telephone: 802-464-3759
Rooms: Nine, each with private bath.
Rates: $50 to $60, MAP, per person, double occupancy. Deposits required; the total for one night's visit, or 50% of the total for extended stays. The deposit will be forfeited if you arrive after the date specified, or depart before the final day. Deposits are not refundable, but on 14-days' notice prior to arrival, and for cancellations within the 14-day period, deposits can be credited toward another stay if, and only if, the room can be resold.
Facilities: Open all year. Breakfast for house guests, lunch, dinner. Dining room, terrace, carriage house. Cross-country skiing from inn door, hiking, photo gallery, sugar house, trout pond, wine cellar, tennis. Accessible to wheelchairs. Game bird farm.

High on a windy hill facing Haystack Mountain, you will find a unique and heartwarming country inn, The Hermitage. The owner is a man for all seasons who knows what he is doing. He also has a certain charm, maybe it is the quick smile or a fleeting twinkle as he says ☞ "No piped-in music in *my* inn." You might, though, find a classical guitarist some night, or someone at the piano in the lounge.

Come in the very early spring, and you will find maple sugaring going full blast. There are four sugar houses on the property, and Jim McGovern makes 700 gallons of maple syrup in an unexceptional year. In summer the big kettles are kept simmering, making homemade jams and jellies. Along with this talent for making the most of nature's bounty, Jim is an oenophile (wine lover), has a ☞ wine cellar with a stock of 30,000 bottles. You are never at a loss for the perfect wine to enjoy with this inn's first-rate food.

There are four separate dining rooms. No more than 20 people can be accommodated in each room, so there is a feeling of intimacy, each place providing for quiet conversation while you enjoy a beautiful dinner. The Vermont marble terrace with its gay umbrellas is the right spot for a bit of lunch. The fruit and cheese plate couldn't be better, with five kinds of excellent cheese and five fresh fruits. Jamison, a friendly English setter, may come by to say hello, but he is likely to be distracted by a passing gaggle of geese, and they *will* fly off in a flurry of wings.

The comfortable rooms, four with their own fireplaces, are furnished with antiques and, oh, those brass beds. In the carriage house you will even find a sauna.

How to get there: Wilmington is in southern Vermont, on Route 100, and The Hermitage is on Coldbrook Road.

🍸

E: *The wine cellar. with its two crystal chandeliers, marvelous selection of wine and gifts, turned me on. What to do with your old claw-footed bath tub? Use it to store wine. There is also an old bassinet used for the same purpose.*

Nutmeg Inn
Wilmington, Vermont
05363

Innkeepers: Joan and Rich Combes
Telephone: 802-464-3351
Rooms: Nine, four with private bath.
Rates: $29 to $34, EPB, double occupancy in summer, $32 to $34, EPB, per person in winter.
Facilities: Closed November to mid-December, April and May. Breakfast always, and dinner in winter only, but there are a lot of good places to eat nearby. BYOB bar.

Wilmington has quite a few country inns, and nice ones. It is understandable, with so many lovely old houses placed here and there through the village and hills.

The Nutmeg was originally an early American Vermont farmhouse. In 1957 the farm house was taken over, restored and remodeled into a small country inn. None of the original charm was lost. The rooms, though small, are neat, very clean and fully comfortable. The whole inn reflects ☛ Joan's tidy habits.

Food is hearty and homemade, prepared by the innkeepers themselves. A great country breakfast is available daily.

After a day at the Marlboro Music Festival in the summer, or a day of skiing Mount Snow in the winter, it is nice to relax in the lounge that once was a carriage house. But music and skiing are not all. You have an 18-hole golf course at Mount Snow, tennis at hand, hiking, or just browsing. You have a BYOB bar with piano, TV, and a fireplace.

How to get there: Wilmington is in southern Vermont. The inn is on Route 9, one mile west of the traffic light in town.

Ä

E: *I love old houses. This one is over 200 years old and has a real Vermont tin roof.*

*The glowing carriage lamp beside the door
of a country inn when viewed through a cold rain
erases the rigors of the day
and promises a fine, fine evening.*

On the Rocks Lodge
Wilmington, Vermont
05363

Innkeepers: Orla and Margie Larson
Telephone: 802-464-8364
Rooms: 15, 13 with private bath.
Rates: $42.50 per person, MAP, double occupancy.
Facilities: Closed mid-October to Thanksgiving, and April 15
    to mid-June. Swimming pool, tennis courts, golf near-
    by, cross-country trails and downhill skiing, game
    room, and library. Breakfast and dinner, bar.

If you decide to go hiking or skiing on any of the inn's
18 miles of cross-country trails, a good idea is to take Rockey,
the inn's Great Dane. If you get lost you need only say,
"Rockey, let's go home," and he will take you. Licke, a
Maine coon cat, is a beauty.
    When you enter the living room you look out on the
🖝 heated pool and onto Mount Snow in the background.
🖝 Breathtaking! Off the dining room is a bright and cheery
bar where I have had good fun with some inn guests when I
was here last.

234

☛ Margie is the chef, and she turns out fine gourmet dining, some of the best in New England. All vegetables are fresh, and in summer the salads come from the inn garden. Orla meanwhile maintains an excellent wine cellar.

The rooms all overlook the gardens, and each has a view of the mountains. ☛ All are individually decorated with designer fabrics and wallpapers, in addition to color-coordinated towels and other great personal touches that make this inn very special.

The large couch in the living room is bright, flowered chintz, and nearby is a chess table. The whole room is a delight, with tremendous views any season of the year.

How to get there: From the only traffic light in Wilmington, go north on Route 100, 4.2 miles to a right fork in the road. Turn right and go approximately 1,000 feet, over a bridge, and take your first right. Continue about 2,000 feet, turn left, and go up the hill. The inn is about one-quarter of a mile up, the first place on the left past the Trail's End Lodge.

E: *This is one inn I could move right into and stay, getting fatter and fatter as time passed. But what a way to go.*

The crackle of an inn's hearth
can melt the chilliest of minds and bodies.

Olive Metcalf

The Red Shutters Inn
Wilmington, Vermont
05363

Innkeepers: Loretta Klutsch and Charles Jones
Telephone: 802-464-3768
Rooms: 11, seven with private baths.
Rates: $40, double occupancy, EPB.
Facilities: Closed one week at the end of April and after foliage season in the fall. Breakfast and dinner. Bar. TV in sitting room.

The first time I saw the inn it was snowing, a beautiful sight with the inn nestled up on a rolling hillside among the pines, maples, and apple trees. The inn is a slate-roofed colonial. The grounds are well manicured and complete with vegetable gardens and a brook.

This is a chef-owned inn, and you know this usually means good food. It certainly does here. Charlie has it all in his head and cooks everything from scratch using the ☛ best and freshest foods available.

A very neat bar and lounge can be found right off the living room. The dining room is cozy and has a crackling fireplace, as does the sitting room and the cocktail lounge.

The rooms are comfortable and have private and semi-private baths.

Mount Snow is at hand for skiing, and nearby you will find lakes, tennis, racquet ball and golf. Summer theater and the Marlboro Music Festival are all here. The village itself has quaint shops, ☛ just great for browsers.

How to get there: From I-91 at Brattleboro take Route 9 to Wilmington. The inn is just past the light in the center of the village. It is on your right.

🔔

E: *The names of the animals at the inn are great: Puss Nips, the cat, and Rasberry Sundae, a very friendly Doberman.*

Olive Metcalf

Schroder Haus
Wilmington, Vermont
05363

Innkeepers: Jeff and Kathy Novy
Telephone: 802-464-5574
Rooms: 14, 10 with private bath.
Rates: $25 per person, EP; $37 per person, MAP.
Facilities: Closed in mud season only. Breakfast and dinner.
  BYOB. One suite with fireplace. Skiing, game room and
  sauna.

An inn that serves me ☞ hot, mulled wine after a day in the snow has to be doing something right. If snowmobiles are your thing, they have them up here, with good fields for varooming about across from the inn. Skiing, whether downhill or cross-country, is just minutes away at Hay Stack or Mount Snow.

A sauna feels so good after all these sports. It's the perfect relaxation just before mixing your own cocktails and relaxing in front of a crackling fire. Dinner is a candlelight affair, a nice way to end a day.

Summertime fun includes golf at two championship

courses, tennis, museums, music, shopping, fishing, and trails for walking or hiking.

Wilmington is a special spot in Vermont's lovely land-scape. While it is a great skiing center, it is also a wonderful place any season of the year. This inn, plus the many other good inns in the area, make it a perfect stop for that get-away few days we all need in this hectic world.

How to get there: Take Route 100 north from Wilmington to Higley Hill Road. Turn right up the hill to the inn.

☖☖☖

E: *The animals' names are great. The three cats are Friskey, Mew and Sashay. The dogs are Gatsby and Nori. They are fine Samoyeds.*

If I ever find an inn that bakes fresh macaroons daily,
I shall rent a room for a hundred years.

Olive Metcalf

The White House
Wilmington, Vermont
05363

Innkeeper: Robert Grinold
Telephone: 802-464-2135
Rooms: Eight, all with private bath. One suite.
Rates: $32 to $42.50 per person, MAP.
Facilities: Closed April and May. Breakfast, dinner and Sunday brunch. Skiers lunch in winter. Bar, swimming pool, cross-country skiing and rental center.

The menu reads like one you would expect to find in the White House, full of mouth-watering goodies served in two dining rooms, both of which are 🖝 very elegant. There is also a small, private dining room.

Looking out one side of the inn you see rose gardens with a fountain, and below this is a 🖝 60-foot swimming pool. The grounds are well-groomed, and a pleasure to gaze upon.

There are 18 miles of cross-country trails right here, which also make for wonderful walking in non-snow seasons. The inn has its own ski rental center, in addition to a large apres-ski room open in the winter.

You have your choice of two bars. My favorite is on a large enclosed porch with hanging plants and skylights. The comfortable bar stools go well with the congenial bartender. Watching the snow fall on one of the skylights in the bar is very pretty.

The duck served here is beautifully presented. At the table the rib cage is lifted off and you have a nice ☛ boneless duck served with extra sauce that all ducks need.

As you walk through the gallery on the main floor you are looking at extremely ☛ unusual wallpaper that was printed in Paris in 1912. Add all of these things together, and you have a really good inn for year-round enjoyment.

How to get there: From Route I-91 take Route 9 to Wilmington. The inn is on your right just before you reach the town.

E: *Intrigue! Why did the original owner of the house put in ☛ a secret staircase? You will have to ask where it is.*

The warmth of a country inn
can only be likened to
a well-made down comforter.

241

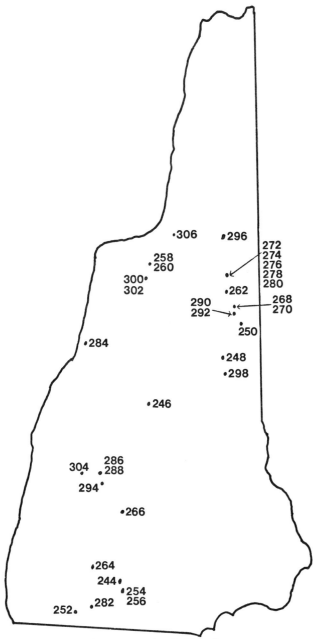

•306   ◦296

                        272
                        274
            258   276
            260   278
                        280
    300•
    302   •262   268
                        270
        290   •◦
        292◦   •
                •
                250
•284

            •248
            •298

        •246

        286
    304• •288
    294 •

        •266

        •264
    244•
            •254
            256
252• •282

numbers on map refer to page numbers in this book

New Hampshire

olive Metcalf

David's
Bennington, New Hampshire
03442

Innkeeper: David Glynn
Telephone: 603-588-2458
Rooms: Two, with private bath.
Rates: $35, double occupancy.
Facilities: Closed in January, February, and March, and on
   Mondays. Breakfast for house guests only, lunch and
   dinner. Liquor license. Parking. Entertainment on Sat-
   urday night.

We think that David can feed about 40 people, but he
has overnight accommodations for only four, if they are
friendly. The rooms with their beamed ceilings are cozy and
charming. David is known for his food, locally and also far
and wide. If you want to go on Saturday night reserve way,
way ahead, because ☞ Nora Lee Sysyn will be singing and
playing the piano, which causes many other people to start
singing, and you know what that leads to.
   The house belonged to David's grandmother, and he is
still working on restoration. The lady who was doing interior

stencils died before she was quite finished, but the stencils remain and work continues. The wide, board floors are original, and even some of the plaster is, too. The house was originally built in 1788, moved in 1838, then moved to the present location in 1928. We hope it has settled for good.

The food is all home-cooked, and you should enjoy it. You will also like this little crossroads of a town and will quickly discover that David has a finger in almost every pie in town, though the ☛ lobster and country chicken pies at the inn are the best.

How to get there: Going north, exit from I-91 at Brattleboro and take Route 5 north to Route 9. Stay on 9 until North Branch, then turn right onto Route 31, which will take you into Bennington. You will probably spot David's Antique Shop first, and David's Restaurant and Inn is just across the street.

E: *The old carriage seat in the tiny sitting room intrigues me. From the Surrey with the fringe on top?*

Olive Metcalf

The Pasquaney Inn
Bridgewater, New Hampshire
03222

Innkeepers: Mary and Jim Shipe
Telephone: 603-744-2712
Rooms: Summer 28, winter 18, 10 with private bath.
Rates: $25 to $32.50. Special packages for groups.
Facilities· Closed October 15 to May 15 unless ski conditions
    permit opening. Breakfast and dinner in the winter, on
    weekends only, or for three or more guests. Swimming,
    shuffleboard, croquet, badminton, lawn bowling, horse
    shoes, skiing, fishing and hiking. Summer breakfast and
    dinner.

The sideboard in the lobby of the inn is a 1790 Balti-
more Hepplewhite, a thing of beauty. The living room, with
a fireplace, looks out over Newfound Lake, as does the dining
room. Dining at the inn is informal and relaxed, with all
meals served family-style. ☛ Vegetables, always fresh,
come from either the inn's ample gardens or the local mar-
kets. Best of all, the desserts and the breads are all done in the
inn's own pastry kitchen.

246

Guest rooms are bright and attractive, some with a lake view, and the others with great views of the surrounding mountains. There are private and shared baths, and be sure to specify your wants when you make a reservation.

Basically Pasquaney is a family inn, with children always welcome. The recreation barn has a basketball court, shuffleboard courts, Ping-Pong and a full, square, dance floor with an old-fashioned caller's balcony. There is a calico cat called Mother Cat, and two other felines called simply Cat.

There is much to do here, no matter what season of the year. The inn has its own sandy beach on the lovely lake, also little skiffs for those who wish to take a row around the cove. Sailboats can be rented nearby. Golf and tennis are also near at hand. Winter brings skiing, spring means fishing for land-locked salmon or trout, and fall is that glorious foliage season. Newfound Lake is very reminiscent of the lake district of northern England, and beautiful.

How to get there: Go up I-93, exit left onto Route 104, then right onto Route 3A. The inn is on the right across from Newfound Lake.

E: *The inn prepares box lunches for hikers, skiers and motor trippers. Nice touch*

Stafford's in the Fields
Chocorua, New Hampshire
03817

Innkeepers: Ramona & Fred Stafford
Telephone: 603-323-7766
Rooms: Eight, two with private bath. Cottages.
Rates: In summer, $45 to $49, MAP, per person, double occupancy.
Facilities: Closed April and May, and November to December 26. Breakfast and dinner for house guests. Parking. Clay tennis courts.

Stafford's in the Fields is an impossible collection of contradictory things that add up to an enchanting place to bring your tired mind, body, and jaded palate. The inn keepers will fix them up good as new. Several years ago the Staffords transplanted themselves from California to this wonderful old farm, (part of the house is almost 200 years old), settled in with the children, and they are still working to make it the most engaging and different place on the Eastern seaboard.

Where to begin? The barn. On Sunday nights in

summer there is a string quartet. The barn's acoustics are remarkable. On Thursday nights there is square dancing. The children are still here, growing up. The daughter of the house is responsible for the really sinful desserts.

Ramona Stafford likes to cook in a sort of French country style, with wine and spices and herbs, fresh vegetables, and all of it *only* for guests. And if she thinks it will go well, she might even throw a little Mexican dinner. Breakfasts are scrumptious, and eggs Benedict or waffles are served on Sunday. Omelettes are available most any day, and what a choice! There is sour cream with green chiles, mild country cheddar, or cheddar and salsa. Eggs come any style, direct from Ramona's own chickens.

Fred Stafford says there is an inexhaustible supply of ☞ "nature things to do." Just sitting, watching the swallows swoop, or a leaf spin slowly to the ground, restores what you've lost in today's busy world. Look at a mountain, play croquet, breathe that unpolluted air.

Turn in the lane some snowy evening and see Stafford's glowing in the field, waiting to welcome you to a world well lost. They feature cross-country skiing on their own trails.

How to get there: Take I-93 north from Concord, Route 104 to Meredith, then Route 25 to Whittier, and Route 113 to Chocorua. Before you get into Chocorua look along the left, and you will find a little road that will bring you to Stafford's. Coming south from Conway take Route 16, and turn right in Chocorua. The inn road will be on your right.

♔

E: *Bulah, a Brittany spaniel, and Thomas the cat, are the chief animals in residence. It's heartwarming to see the wagging tail and hear the purr in welcome.*

Darby Field Inn
Conway, New Hampshire
03818

Innkeepers: Marc and Marily Donaldson
Telephone: 603-447-2181
Rooms: 11 nine with private bath.
Rates: $32 to $38 per person, MAP, double occupancy.
Facilities Closed in April. Breakfast and dinner except Tuesdays. Bar, television, swimming pool, library, skiing, and hiking.

Set high atop Bald Hill in New Hampshire's White Mountains, and complete with spectacular views, is Darby Field Inn. Located 1,000 feet above Mount Washington Valley and only 1½ miles from Conway, the inn has a lot going for it.

Dining is a delight here. Dinners are elegantly served by candlelight as the sun sets over Mount Washington Valley. ☛ The view from the dining room is incredible, and the fine food served here is also unforgettable.

On a snowy winter night the huge cobblestone fireplace downstairs is the center of warm conversation, and if you want a livelier time, come into the pub where there is music and fun for everyone.

The rooms are charming, some with four-poster beds. All are comfortable as inn rooms could be.

There is so much to do in this area and it would be impossible for anyone, anytime of year, to say they were bored. Conway is close by, and its shopping is fun.

How to get there: Turn on Bald Hill Road a half mile south of the Kancamagus Highway on Route 16, then go one mile up the hill and turn right onto a dirt road. The inn is one mile beyond, on your right.

E: ☞ *The bathrooms in this mountain-top inn are tucked away in ingenious fashions. Imagine an ell-shaped shower!*

> *A good innkeeper, a good cook,*
> *and an affable barkeeper*
> *are as standard in a country inn*
> *as a fire engine in a fire house*

olive Metcalf

Fitzwilliam Inn
Fitzwilliam, New Hampshire
03447

Innkeepers: Charles & Barbara Wallace
Telephone: 603-585-9000
Rooms: 22, 12 baths.
Rates: $16 to $24 EP.
Facilities: Open every day of the year. Breakfast, lunch, dinner, bar. TV, swimming pool, sauna, skiing.

"The more plastic motels that are built, the more people are going to be driven back to a warm country inn, without wall-to-wall carpeting, but with something else." Enoch Fuller said this. And the Fitzwilliam Inn, which he owned and operated until his death in 1973, is indeed a warm country inn. The Fitzwilliam Inn is still the same old-fashioned New England inn that has been offering food, grog, and lodging to weary travelers since 1796.

If sleigh riding is your idea of a great winter sport, book yourself in at Fitzwilliam. ☛ In summer there is square dancing in the village, and there are also 12 antique shops in this little town. The bar is a great little taproom, where hot winter drinks are called Broken Legs. Meals are hearty New England affairs, with a wonderful homemade pumpkin bread, and homemade desserts. All menus are tacked to little bread boards.

The Wallaces like to have music at the inn, so there are concerts every Sunday in the winter, and on special occasions. In summer you can enjoy the beautiful pool, after the sauna, and then lunch on the patio. All this, with the charm of a centuries-old inn, lovely antiques, and a cordial welcome from the innkeeper.

The men's room is a must. It has a blackboard for graffiti and a great red rocking chair for relaxing.

How to get there: The inn is 205 miles from New York, 65 miles from Boston at the intersection of routes 12 and 119. Vermont Transit buses stop at the door.

E: *Over the fireplace hangs this word puzzle. The Wallaces will have to unscramble it for you.*

> *If the B mt put:*
> *If the B. putting:*
> *Don't put: over A - der*
> *You'd be an ★ it!*

Olive Metcalf

The Inn at Crotched Mountain
Francestown, New Hampshire
03043

Innkeepers: John and Rose Perry
Telephone: 603-588-6840
Rooms: Nine, four with private bath.
Rates: $25 single, to $40, EP, double occupancy.
Facilities: Closed first three weeks in November, and on Sunday and Monday for dining. No lunch in winter. Breakfast, lunch and dinner, bar. Parking, pool, clay tennis court. Wonderful scenery. Pets allowed, $2 each.

This 150-year-old colonial house is located on the northern side of Crotched Mountain. There is a 40-mile view of the Piscataquog Valley, complete with spacious skies. Both innkeepers have gone to ☛ school to learn their trade, and what a charming house to practice it in. They are both pretty special themselves. Rose is from Singapore, and John is a Yankee.

Come and stay, there is lots to do. There are three golf courses in the nearby valley, fishing is great, there is a wading pool for the young, as well as a 30' by 60' pool for real swimmers. Two areas provide skiing, one at the front door, and another down the road. Two clay tennis courts eliminate that tiresome waiting for a playing area. And come evening there are two summer theaters, one at Peterborough and another in Milford.

How to get there: Only 75 miles from Boston, take Route 128 from Boston to Route 3. Turn left onto 101A, then right onto Route 13. Turn left at New Boston and that will take you into Francestown. Continue after turning right onto Mountain Road (Route 47) and the inn is on the left.

E: *Any house that has nine fireplaces needs a wood lot and a man with a chain saw. Three of the bedrooms here have a fireplace, so remember to request one when you reserve.*

*The register of a country inn
is a treasure of the names of good people.*

The Inn at Tory Pines
Francestown, New Hampshire
03043

Innkeepers: Dick Tremblay and Jack Sullivan
Telephone: 603-588-6352
Rooms: 28, two suites, all with private bath.
Rates: $42.50 to $49 EP, double occupancy, but check for package deals.
Facilities: Open all year, breakfast, lunch and dinner. Bar, TV, swimming pool, golf, downhill and cross-country skiing, ice skating, golf pro shop, skiing pro shop, tennis.

The inn is the home of the ☛ Hall of Fame golf course, which is patterned after the best 18 holes from famous courses all over the world. Dick Tremblay is a PGA professional golfer. They have carts, lessons, clinics and a good practice range.

Skiing is also superb here. The inn is at the foot of Crotched Mountain in the Monadnock region of southern New Hampshire. There are excellent cross-country trails on over 400 acres of the inn's own land plus ☛ guided mountain tours for the more adventurous. Complete rental equipment is available, along with waxing and repair services.

The three dining rooms are extremely well-furnished and comfortable. Two have fireplaces, and one of them has those great Indian shutters on the windows that fold back completely out-of-sight. The house is old, built in 1799. It is a Georgian colonial. The bar has a 14' long pine top cut from one log, plus a fireplace. The lounge also has a huge fireplace. There is even a private dining room upstairs.

Food here is excellent. I had broiled scallops that the chef had made more than somewhat special, as he does with almost all of his dishes. The stuffed shrimp were huge. Eating my way through New England sure is fun, even if a bit fattening.

The rooms are across the road in what once was an old barn, but today you would never know it. All the rooms are super comfortable with great views. Two big maples, exactly as old as the house, flank the original entrance. They are called "wedding maples."

How to get there: From Hartford, take I-91 north to Brattleboro, to Route 101 east to Peterborough, New Hampshire. Then take Route 202 north to Bennington, New Hampshire and take Route 47. Tory Pines is four miles farther on the left. From Boston, take Route 3 to 101A west to Milford, New Hampshire, then a hard right at the rotary to Route 13 to New Boston, New Hampshire, and Route 136 to Francestown, New Hampshire. Bear right in the village. The inn is four miles, on right, on Route 47.

E: *In the pond where you skate live a gaggle of geese and two ducks. The inn also has a pony whose name is Dusty.*

257

Olive Metcalf

The Horse and Hound
Wells Road
Franconia, New Hampshire
03580

Innkeepers: Sybil & Bob Carey
Telephone: 603-823-5501
Rooms: Eight, with private bath.
Rates: $35 to $50, EP, double occupancy.
Facilities: Closed mid-April to mid-May, and Wednesdays.
Continental breakfast for house guests, dinner, bar.
Skiing, swimming.

When you walk through the door of the inn you are greeted by a small wooden hobby horse with a sign about his neck that says, "No one over 11 will ride me." Children are welcome at the inn only if well behaved and supervised at all times.

The rooms here are bright, airy, and color-coordinated, with nice views on all sides and ☛ fresh fruit to welcome you.

Chamber music is played throughout the dinner hour.

Bob was in broadcasting and truly has an electronic closet full of music. Dinner here is a gourmet's delight. The menu changes frequently, and dinners are prepared using house wines. For entrees there are treats such as duckling with apples, veal many different ways, Beef Bourguignonne, interesting fish and vegetables. For starters, try a spinach crepe with warm horseradish mayonnaise. I can taste it even now. All the baking is done at the inn.

There's an abundance of plants hanging and sitting in the picture window of the bar and lounge. You will also find a small but excellent library here.

How to get there: Take I-93 north, exit at Route 18, and turn left. The inn is on the left, several miles down the road.

E: *One of the few funnies from Nixon's term is hanging on a wall near the ladies lounge. You must go and see it.*

A good inn, good food, a warm bed and a loving woman . . . heaven can be another time.

259

Olive Metcalf

Lovett's by Lafayette Brook
Franconia, New Hampshire
03580

Innkeepers: Mr. & Mrs. Charles J. Lovett, Jr.
Telephone: 603-823-7761
Rooms: Seven in main house, plus cottages and dorm.
Rates: $38 to $40, MAP, per person.
Facilities: Closed after Columbus Day until December 26,
April, May, and until the third Friday in June. Break-
fast, dinner, bar. Swimming in the pond or pool, game
room, tennis, golf, riding, bicycling, fishing, skiing.

There are a lot of reasons for coming to The White
Mountains and Franconia Notch, and one of the best reasons
is this inn. It was constructed circa 1784, even before a road
was built through Franconia Notch. The inn is well into its
second generation of ☛ one family ownership, and that
says a lot.

Charlie Lovett runs a fine inn. As he says, we work hard
at having the best table and best cellar in the North Country.
The menu changes daily. Some of the favorites are lamb
served with their own chutney, veal and mushrooms, egg-

plant with caviar, fresh shrimp mousse, and, at breakfast, sour cream cheddar cheese omelets or shirred eggs with fresh mushrooms. These are but a few of the delights that Charlie comes up with. The inn has its own herb garden. At last count there were 37 different herbs at hand. No wonder the food is so good. Desserts, as you would expect, are heavenly.

There is a lovely terrace overlooking the mountains and the pool. Actually there are two pools. One is solar heated and the other fed from mountain springs. Oh, to be that hale and hearty for the latter.

A new addition to the area of Franconia Notch is the New England Ski Museum, an excellent review of a sport that goes back 5,000 years. It is important to preserve these rare artifacts.

How to get there: Take I-93 north, exit at Route 18 and turn left. The inn is on your right.

E: *The bar, the bar! From the staircase in a Newport Mansion, the marble bar is the most inviting spot I've run into in a month of Sundays.*

I never thought of business when awakened at an inn by the three o'clock chime of a nearby church.

Bernerhof Inn
Glen, New Hampshire
03838

Innkeepers: Ted and Sharon Wroblewski
Telephone: 603-383-4414
Rooms: Nine, one with private bath.
Rates: $17.50 per person, including breakfast.
Facilities: Closed November through Christmas, and mid-April to Memorial Day. Breakfast for house guests, lunch, dinner, bar, sauna.

Fine European cuisine in the old-world tradition is what Ted and Sharon consider their outstanding food to be. Specialities include Weiner Schnitzel, Holstein Schnitzel, and even Schnitzel Cordon Bleu. Their desserts should be outlawed. Cherries Jubilee or Meringue Glace are two of my fattening favorites, but delicious. They have an excellent wine list, and coffees for the gourmet finish.

Though some of the rooms are rather small, they are all clean, light, airy, and have new mattresses and box springs. These things I think are important to any inn.

The living room has a very unusual tall, round coal

stove and a wonderful electronic machine. I hate electronics but I make an exception for the "Piano Corder," an ingenious tape-playing gadget that plays the inn's Steinway. It is much more clever than the old pianos that played rolls.

The bar and lounge is called the "Zumstein Room," and it is a charming place, serving some real unusual food, like cheese fondues, Delice de Gruyere, Raclette, and always a quiche du jour.

You are but a few minutes from either North Conway or Jackson, so you will not lack for something to do absolutely any month of the year.

How to get there: From North Conway take Route 16 north. At Glen, turn left onto Route 302. The inn is on your right.

❦

E: *A free champagne breakfast in bed is yours on the third morning of your stay. It comes with eggs benedict and fresh flowers. My. My.*

> *"The righteous minds of innkeepers*
> *Induce them now and then,*
> *To crack a bottle with a friend*
> *Or treat unmoneyed men."*
> G. K. Chesterton

Olive Metcalf

The John Hancock Inn
Hancock, New Hampshire
03449

Innkeepers: Glynn & Pat Wells
Telephone: 603-525-3318
Rooms: 10, all with bath.
Rates: $33.50, EP, single; to $38.50, double occupancy.
Facilities: Closed one week in early spring, one week in late fall. Breakfast, lunch, dinner, lounge. Parking. Swimming at pond, bicycles loaned, tennis

Operated as an inn since 1789, the John Hancock has new, young owners, the Wells family. Carefully preserved is The Mural Room, believed to date back to the early years of the inn. The Carriage Lounge is very unusual, with tables made from giant bellows from an old foundry in Nova Scotia. Seats are made from old buggy seats. The name stems from the fact that John Hancock, the founding father, once owned most of the land that comprises the present town of Hancock. Set among twisting hills with a weathered clapboard facade, graceful white pillars, and a warm red door, the inn represents all that is good about old inns. Warm welcomes, good food, sound drinks, and good beds, set in a quiet town that hasn't changed much in the last two centuries.

Dinner is served by candlelight, and when winter storms howl through the hills the fireplace in the bar has a crackling fire to warm your heart and toes. Braided rugs cover part of the wide board floors, and primitive paintings hang on the walls.

Swim in summer in Norway Pond, within walking distance of the inn. Climb mountains, or just sit and listen to the church chimes during foliage time. Alpine and cross-country skiing are nearby in winter. Or browse in the antique shops on a cool spring morn.

How to get there: From Boston take Route 128, then Route 3 to 101 west. Hancock is located just off Route 202, above Peterborough.

E: *The inn dog is a Lhasa named Nay-Daak Poo, which means "little innkeeper."*

*We sat together round a single table and talked
and heard each other in the quiet of the inn.*

Olive Metcalf

Colby Hill Inn
Henniker, New Hampshire
03242

Innkeepers: The Glover Family
Telephone: 603-428-3281
Rooms: Eight, four with private bath.
Rates: $27 to $38, EP. $15 deposit required to confirm reservation.
Facilities: Open all year. Breakfast and dinner, except on Monday. Bar, parking. TV, swimming.

This picturesque old house dates back to 1800. It leans and dips a bit here and there, but that only adds to the charm. The ☞ wide floor boards are authentic. You cannot find boards like that nowadays. Don Glover, Jr., is chief innkeeper. He supervises the cooking and everything else that needs doing in a country inn. While researching this book I have found innkeepers up in trees, down in cellars, chopping wood, and even doing dishes. Don can be found at any one of these activities.

Don's parents have come up from New Jersey to help out at the inn. He also has a young wife and a young son, still a bit small for any duties. To make a complete inn family, there is Tar, the inn dog, who can nearly lose his tail with each welcome he gives guests.

The meals are simple and delicious, with steak or chicken served many ways, fresh seafood, including salmon, and very good desserts, like lemon curd and chocolate mousse. The inn has its own garden, plus the use of the next door neighbor's garden, so in season there are a wealth of fresh vegetables.

Henniker is a small New England college town. Indeed, New England College is here. For skiers there is Pat's Peak and Sunapee, which is also a state park. Cross-country trails abound in every direction, supplying every type of skiing and scenery.

How to get there: Go up I-91 to Brattleboro. Take Route 9 east into Henniker.

E: *The lounge is new. Come and see it.*

With its swinging sign near
the hills it stands,
Vine-clad and filled with cheer.

'Tis a place to laze through
fresh, golden days
with sunlit peaks so near,

So good-bye to cares,
this spot is rare,
and we thank kind fate
for having brought us here.

The New England Inn
Intervale, North Conway, New Hampshire
03845

Innkeepers: Linda and Joe Johnston
Telephone: 603-356-5541
Rooms: 50, all with private bath, cottages with fireplaces.
Rates: $27 to $64 MAP, double occupancy.
Facilities: Closed April and November. Breakfast and dinner, three clay tennis courts, swimming and wading pools, cross-country from the inn, entertainment on weekends and holidays, conference room, lighted night cross-country ski trails.

The Johnston family looked over some 25 inns before deciding on The New England Inn for their dream-come-true of owning a country inn.

A landmark for travelers for nearly 170 years, The New England Inn started as a farm in the early 1800's. Today it is one of our real fine inns, full of antiques and old pine paneling. And the Johnstons are always looking for ways to make the inn even better.

The Intervale Tavern offers a blazing fire, a fully

stocked bar, dancing and live entertainment. The Tavern, from earliest times, was a club for locals and travelers to meet, have drinks, and indulge in interesting conversation.

The food is outstanding. ☞ Chef Sam has been here for well over 30 years, and his old-fashioned Yankee cooking includes steak, lobster, prime ribs, and ☞ baked sugar-cured ham with raisin sauce. Hot apple crisp is my publisher's favorite food, and it is done scrumptiously. You can add hot Indian pudding to any of the great things served here. Each meal is enhanced with ☞ piping hot rolls from the inn's own ovens.

Five-course dinners are standard. What a way to go. By the way, the dining room has a unique name. It is called Anna Martin's to honor a former owner.

The New England Inn cross-country learning center is complete, and makes this great sport what it should be: fun and easy. ☞ Night skiing by romantic moonlight through quiet field and wood is an unforgettable experience.

How to get there: The inn is at the Gateway to the White Mountains, on Resort Loop, Route 16A, 3½ miles north of North Conway.

E: *The Tavern serves nice hot chili, good stews, and fresh quiche. I cannot forget the inn animals, Barny the cat, and Brandy the dog.*

olive Metcalf

Tuckermans Inn
Intervale, New Hampshire
03845

Innkeepers: Hugh and Marjorie Osborn
Telephone: 603-356-2752
Rooms: Ten, four with private bath.
Rates: $36 to $40, double occupancy with breakfast; also midweek package rates.
Facilities: Open all year. Dining room closed Tuesdays in winter. Breakfast and dinner. Tavern. In winter brunch on Saturday and Sunday.

The old, original chimney and fireplace with its brick oven in the dining room form a beehive construction the size of an entire room in the middle of the house. This was all built in 1785 by Captain Elijah Dinsmore. Records indicate that Captain Dinsmore received a license "to keep a Publik House" in 1795. In addition to being a publik house, the lovely old inn served also as a stage coach stop.

Tuckermans has been newly renovated and restored to provide first-class accommodations with fine dining year-round.

A special note on Tucks Tavern, which is done in the eighteenth century tradition. The bar is a very long slab of wood cut from a single tree. There are booth seats and ☛ a wood-burning stove to make it all very cozy.

The dining rooms, all with marvelous views, serve excellent food. The Tavern menu is unique. ☛ "That old bread Magic" is certainly a different way to list the sandwiches, among which you will find the Salad Bag, which is fresh spinach salad served in Syrian Pita bread with a melted cheese topping and Tucks dressing. Or how about a Sorry Charlie which is a surprise, and I promised to keep it that way by not telling you what is in it. It is also served in Syrian Pita and is well worth your trying. Dinners are highly recommended, especially the fancy ☛ continental veal served six ways.

How to get there: Take Route 16 north out of North Conway. The inn is on the left, just before you come to Route 16A.

♆

E: *The inn dog is a little white poodle called Benji.*

"There is nothing which has been contrived by man by which so much happiness is produced as by a good tavern or inn."
—Samuel Johnson

Christmas Farm Inn
Jackson, New Hampshire
03846

Innkeepers: Bill & Sydna Zeliff
Telephone: 603-383-4313
Rooms: 27, 24 with private bath. Also a 1771 saltbox, a sugar house which includes a two-room suite, and bunk rooms in the main inn for up to four persons.
Rates: $36 to $45, MAP. Write for special weekly rates.
Facilities: Open all year. Dining room closed in November, April, and May. Sugar Plum Dining Room, Mistletoe Pub, a living room with TV, large swimming pool, fully-equipped game room, putting green, shuffleboard, 80 miles of cross-country trails, five alpine ski areas within 20 minutes, summer theater at Eastern Slope Play-house, golf, tennis, sauna, complimentary movies.

Yes, Virginia, there is a Christmas Farm Inn, and they have the Mistletoe Pub and the Sugar Plum Dining Room to prove it. The food is fit for any Santa and his helpers, from the hearty, full country breakfast, which includes ☞ home-made doughnuts, muffins, and sticky buns, to gracious dinners that include three entrees each evening, two home-made soups, a full salad bar, homemade breads, and a complete dessert menu.

All of the rooms share Christmas names: Holly, Dasher, Prancer, Vixen, Donner, Cupid, Comet, and Blitzen.

Jackson is in the heart of the White Mountains, so bring your skis, or come in summer for the annual Christmas-in-July Week. ☞ There's a magnificent gala Christmas party Wednesday night with an outside buffet and Christmas tree, as well as live entertainment, dancing, shuffleboad and golf tournaments. Santa must live nearby, because he never fails to arrive in a most unusual manner.

The inn dogs are Christy and Freckles, and they share their domain with Dynamite, the inn cat. These are the real owners, you know.

Flowers are everywhere to warm the eyes on a winter day. There are books, lots of them, in various spots all over the inn. The sugar house is the honeymoon suite, called Santa's Workshop. The ☞ baked goods are so tasty the Zeliff's had to open a small bakery. The sign reads, "Home Sweet, Homemade Baked Goods from our Backdoor Bakery." When you want lunch for skiing, hiking, or whatever, ask for one of Santa's Sack Lunches.

The newest addition to the inn is the 135-year-old barn that has been raised and completely restored. The fireplace is of stone and is 12 feet wide. There is everything out here, a sauna, a bar, couches, Ping-Pong, bumper pool, four suites, a kitchen, and a lovely function center.

How to get there: Go north from Portsmouth, New Hampshire on the Spalding Turnpike (Route 16) all the way to Jackson, which is just above North Conway. At Jackson is a covered bridge on your right. Take the bridge through Jackson Village, and up the hill. The inn is a quarter mile beyond the village center.

E: *Lots of elves work here. One real good one is Ellie Fernald, the baking elf, and you must taste her sweets to believe them.*

Dana Place Inn
3 Pinkham Notch Road,
Jackson, New Hampshire
03846

Innkeepers: Betty & Malcolm Jennings
Telephone: 603-383-6822
Rooms: 14, eight baths to share, some private baths.
Rates: $20 to $26, per person, double occupancy; $24 to $35,
EPB per person, single.
Facilities: Closed late October to mid-December, and mid-
April to mid-June. Breakfast for house guests, dinner,
piano bar. Parking. Swimming, tennis, downhill and
cross-country skiing, fishing.

Located at the foot of Mount Washington, surrounded
by 600,000 acres of unspoiled National Forest, the Dana
Place Inn nestles in a beautiful valley next to the Ellis River.
The house was built in the mid-nineteenth century and
surely must have been a stage coach stop. We know it was
once a farmhouse, set amid an apple orchard and built by
Antwin Dana. Set your own pace amid lawns, gardens,
streams, meadows, and woodland trails. Walk through the

orchard, past the swimming pool, take the country road past the tennis courts, along a mossy tree-shaded path, through a clearing, and ☞ there is a crystal-clear, rockbound pool in the Ellis River. Peace is beyond description.

Skiing is, of course, superb here, as well as hiking and mountain climbing for the experienced mountaineer. During school vacations lunch can be had at the inn, and in all seasons the kitchen specializes in picnic lunches. Come home to dinner and wonderful New England food, with more than a sophisticated continental touch. ☞ Choose between iced Gazpacho and Aunt Laura's Cold Peach Soup. In summer the vegetables come right out of Dana Place's own garden. Betty Jennings' dad has been chef at The New England Inn in Intervale for 30 years, so she knows about food and inns.

After a day of skiing, the place to unwind is the attractive bar. Enjoy hot buttered rum, hot mulled cider, good cheer, and if it is a weekend, the intimate piano music of Mike Jewell.

How to get there: Take I-95 north to Portsmouth, then the Spaulding Turnpike to Route 16 north at Rochester. Follow Route 16 north past Jackson Village.

E: *The muppets are for sale, along with original watercolors by Myke Morton and David Baker.*

Thorn Hill Lodge
Jackson, New Hampshire
03846

Innkeepers: Donald and Gail Hechtle
Telephone: 603-383-4242
Rooms: 22, 16 with private bath.
Rates: $32 to $45 EP, double occupancy, $30 to $38 EP, single.
Facilities: Closed April 1 to mid-June, November 1 to mid-December. Breakfast, dinner, bar, swimming pool, cross-country skiing from the inn, art workshops.

Mountains are everywhere you look. The inn has a porch with ☞ New England rocking chairs and a view that even on bad days is spectacular.

Donald is the chef, and he has a supper salad on his menu that is hard to beat. I am a real salad nut, so I should know. Every Sunday there is traditional roast New England turkey. It once was chicken every Sunday, but things do change. Speaking of chicken there is ☞ boneless breast of chicken baked with spiced bread crumbs that is laced with honey and bacon. Yum, yum.

In winter there is skiing of all types, and five alpine slopes, three of which are at the inn's doorstep. There are 125 kilometers of good trails at all levels, in addition to a lighted skating pond, and tobogganing or sledding on the inn's own hills. The inn provides trail lunches, a heated waxing room, and baby-sitting.

The Volvo International Tennis Tournament at the end of July is six miles away, in North Conway. Also, Storyland is close by. And an alpine summer slide, the Mount Washington Auto Road, and the Wildcat Mountain Gondola Ride are all at hand. For skiers, there is a shuttle bus service on weekends and holiday weeks that connects all Jackson inns to the slopes. The charge is nominal.

The food at the inn is country cooking, with homemade pastries and fresh baked breads. All goes well with the most accommodating innkeepers.

How to get there: Go north from Portsmouth, New Hampshire on the Spalding Turnpike (Route 16) all the way to Jackson, which is just above North Conway. At Jackson is a covered bridge on your right. Take the bridge, and just one block this side of the village center on the right is Thorn Hill Road, which you take up the hill. The inn is on your right.

☀

E: *There is a neat lounge with a stupendous view. Wish I were there now.*

Olive Metcalf

Whitney's Village Inn
Jackson, New Hampshire
03846

Innkeepers: Darrell Trapp and Bob De Paolo
Telephone: 603-383-6886
Rooms: 36, 30 with private bath. Two cottages with two
  bedrooms, living room, bath, fireplace.
Rates: Winter $33 to $45 per person MAP; summer $33 to
  $69 per person MAP. Package rates available.
Facilities: Closed April and November. Breakfast and dinner,
  plus a Hobo Lunch available. Bar, skiing, ice skating,
  tobogganing, tennis, swimming, library, game room.

It's pretty nice to crawl out of bed, dress, have a sumptuous breakfast and ☞ walk across to the lifts, trails, ski
shop or ski school, all just a snowball's throw away. Black
Mountain is right here. The lifts can handle 2,900 skiers per
hour, so there is hardly any waiting. Fifteen trails serve the
mountain, and all are kept in the best condition possible.

A lighted skating rink is right beside the inn. Bring your
own skates, or rent them here. The inn also has tobogganing,
a sport everyone should try at least once.

The dining room is truly a garden spot, with plants hanging all about, ☞ herbs growing in a large cart to be used by the chef, flower flats on each table for holding salt, pepper, sugar, and a copy of Burpee's Farm Annual. Old Burpee posters are on the walls. Another flower cart holds the salad, another the vegetables, and a fourth the desserts. It's very impressive to look beyond all this and see the skiers arriving at the base of the mountain.

☞ Tea is served at 3:30 every afternoon in the living room. This, too, is where you have your before and after dinner drinks.

The Shovel Handle Lounge is a most unique pub in a beautifully restored barn adjacent to the inn. This barn offers panoramic views of Black Mountain. After skiing, and after dinner, enjoy your favorite beverage served up in ☞ pint Mason jars. Very different. And do join the Pub Mug Club. Bring in your own mug, receive a card and a tee shirt, and then your mug hangs here for your exclusive use. There is a television in the pub for special events, a huge fireplace, and great fun. If you are hungry, the pub's own kitchen can serve you some chili. Or you can read a book, for there is a good library here. There is just no end to the things you can do.

How to get there: Go north from Conway 22 miles on Route 16. Take a right on Route 16B through a covered bridge, through Jackson, and follow signs to the inn.

E: *I love the Hobo Lunch, served continental or American-style in a small burlap bag, plus your choice of either French wine or imported natural fruit juices.*

olive Metcalf

The Wildcat Inn
Jackson, New Hampshire
03846

Innkeepers: Pam and Marty Sweeney
Telephone: 603-383-4245
Rooms: 18, eight with private bath.
Rates: $15 to $18, EP.
Facilities: Closed mid-April to Memorial Day. Full breakfast, lunch, dinner, bar, music in lounge.

The big old front porch has been converted into a dining room. It is sad to lose a porch, but this is such a popular spot the space was needed. Take a look at the menu and you will see why they needed more dining space, with all their ☞ interestingly different, good-tasting food. The ☞ pie crust is the best I ever had, and the fillings they put in them are delicious. All of the desserts are lovingly made by Pam. There are good soups, fine quiches, and chili with a hearty tang. Not just the same old cuisine, the food here will titillate your taste buds.

The Wildcat is a real old-time country inn, but there is nothing old-fashioned about the food or entertainment. In the big, old Tavern with two large fireplaces, you will find live musical entertainment, maybe a flautist, a lutanist, or a classical guitarist. Whatever it may be, you can count on it being good.

The inn is right next to either alpine or cross-country skiing. One-hundred-and-twenty-five kilometers of maintained, well-groomed trails start at the front door, near the touring headquarters, and end in the backyard beside the heated waxing hut. You can get touring skis, boots, alpine ski equipment, and touring instructions just a few strides from the inn's front door. But when the snows melt, you will find these trails glorious for walking or hiking. Jackson is a good spot anytime of year.

How to get there: Take Route 16 north from North Conway. Take Route 16A to your right, through a covered bridge, and into Jackson. The inn is in the center of town.

♍

E: *Five downhill ski areas, with established ski schools only a few minutes away, are pretty nice; so is the inn dog, Sassafras.*

And now once more I shape my way
Thro' rain or shine, thro' thick or thin,
Secure to meet, at close of day
With kind reception, at an inn.
William Shenstone, 1714–1763
(written at an Inn at Henley)

.Olive Metcalf

The Monadnock Inn
Jaffrey Center, New Hampshire
03454

Innkeeper: Sally Roberts
Telephone: 603-532-7001
Rooms: 14, eight share baths.
Rates: $20 to $35, double occupancy, per room.
Facilities: Closed Christmas, open year-round. Continental
    breakfast included in room price, lunch except on Sat-
    urday and Sunday, dinner, bar.

Three sets of innkeepers have operated this inn since
1920. When I researched the first edition of this book in 1973
I discovered the Monadnock Inn, but the owners were planning to sell and retire and asked me not to include it. I am
happy to say that Sally Roberts is the new innkeeper, and
what a terrific job she is doing. The house has been here a
long time, and I hope will be here lots longer.

From the minute you set foot on the wide front porch
until you sink into your comfortable four-poster at night you
will be happy at this lovely inn. There is so much to do. Have
you ever been to the Cathedral in the Pines? It's not far. Have

you ever wanted to get really involved in maple sugaring? This is the place. It can be arranged with a snap of the fingers.

Sally likes to think the Monadnock Inn is capable of taking you back in time. But it was never this good. The food is worth writing home about. The cheesecake, by their own admission, is inn-famous.

In brisk winter weather there is always a roaring fire in one of the fireplaces and miles of cross-country trails for skiers. Or come in the fall for wonderful, glorious foliage. Autumn in New Hampshire should have a song all its own.

How to get there· The inn is located on Route 124, southeast of Keene.

E: *There aren't many places like this around. Cherish it.*

I was lost, I was tired, I was discouraged,
and then I found a friendly inn.

olive Metcalf

Lyme Inn
Lyme, New Hampshire
03768

Innkeepers: Fred & Judy Siemons
Telephone: 603-795-2222
Rooms: 15, nine baths.
Rates: $37 to $52 double occupancy EPB.
Facilities: Closed three weeks after Thanksgiving, and two weeks in late spring. Breakfast, dinner, bar. Dining room closed Tuesday. Parking. TV, library, five rooms with fireplaces.

This lovely inn is on the common of this quiet New Hampshire town. The inn dates back to between 1802 and 1809. All of the original rooms have been restored, in keeping with the age of the building, and each bedroom is filled with antiques and its own unique character. You find stenciled wallpaper, wing chairs, and the huge screened porch comes complete with wicker furniture.

The tavern has a great fireplace, and on a cold night a cheese fondue is a must. ☞ The fresh spinach salad is served with bacon bits and chopped egg, and the house salad dressing is, to quote me, *fan*-tastic. The chef does some wonderful things with fresh seafood, and the desserts served here should be outlawed.

One of our other innkeepers, Esther Serafini, lived here many years ago when she was a young school teacher. Small world!

How to get there: Take Exit 14 from I-91. The inn is located on Route 10, on the village common.

♎

E: *The room that is directly above the taproom has a chaise lounge and is so pretty and charming. All the rooms are lovely, but this is my favorite.*

*A glass of good whiskey
before an open fire in a good inn
is an unspoken toast to life
as it should be lived.*

olive Metcalf

Hide-Away Lodge
New London, New Hampshire
03257

Innkeepers: Lilli & Wolf Heinberg
Telephone: 603-526-4861
Rooms: Eight, with bath.
Rates: EP, $24 daily, $150 weekly; MAP available.
Facilities: Closed Tuesday, open mid-May to November 1.
Fishing and swimming on Lake Sunapee a short walk
away. Excellent golf on three courses, tennis nearby,
summer theater.

There has to be an exception to every rule, and Hide-
Away Lodge is mine. Being open only five months, I feel,
does not qualify an inn for my book . . . until now. I know
you will agree with me. There was no way I could not
include Hide-Away Lodge.

When I drove into this lovely old house and met the
host, Wolf Heinberg, who has a most engaging smile, I knew
I had found something special. Already I had heard about the
food served here, and after talking with Wolf I was sure all I
had heard was true. Thankfully I was able to stay in the last

room in the inn.

Dinner hour arrived, and I went down to the cocktail lounge, The Pipedreaming Pub. I placed a cocktail order, drooled over the menu, ordered dinner, and asked for the wine list. Wolf suggested that maybe a look in the wine cellar would help me decide. I followed him into a huge, temperature-controlled wine cellar. Fantastic, every wall was covered with wine. In the center of the room is a large table with silver candelabras and a beautiful wine book. Wolf is a very proud man, and he should be. The inn carries four stars in the Mobil Guide.

☞ The inn will, on 24-hour notice, and for any number of people, prepare a gourmet feast. Included are pheasant, rack of lamb, venison, and many others. The regular menu is a dream. Crisp duckling with peach glaze is a favorite, not to mention many veal delights, fresh vegetables, and desserts about which I could write a whole chapter. As if this were not enough, there are bits of poetry all over the inn written by Wolf. You must come and read them. But call ahead, reservations are a must.

How to get there: Fly to Lebanon, New Hampshire and be picked up and delivered to the inn. Or by car, follow Main Street past Colby-Sawyer College to the blinker light at the north end of town. Go straight ahead and follow the signs about two miles from town.

⊕

E: *I wanted to stay in the wine cellar.*

olive Metcalf

New London Inn
New London, New Hampshire
03257

Innkeepers: George & Clara Adame
Telephone: 603-526-2791
Rooms: 24, with bath.
Rates: $20 to $25, EP, single; $25 to $35, double.
Facilities: Open all year. Breakfast, lunch, dinner. Breakfast
the only meal served Christmas Day. Nelson's Tavern.
Parking. Skiing, two public beaches nearby.

This inn, which has been serving the traveler since
1792, is blooming anew under the direction of the Adames.
☛ The old inn is full of beautiful antiques. It's worth a trip
to stop and look and eat, even if you can't stay.

New London is the home of Colby Sawyer College.
There is always something going on at the college. Also, the
New London Barn Players is the oldest summer theater in
New Hampshire.

The rooms are nice, large, comfortable, most of them
with cross ventilation and louvered doors. Nelson's Tavern is
a good spot for a quick, light meal. Love the old trunks used

as cocktail tables. The dining room is very gracious. Go and see.

In the summer guests have beach privileges at little Lake Sunapee.

This is a beautiful part of the world any time of year, so come on up.

How to get there: Take Exit 8 at Ascutney, Vermont from I-91. Follow signs to Claremont, New Hampshire. Take Route 11 east to Newport, Sunapee, Georges Mills, and New London. There is bus service via Vermont Transit from Boston, and from White River Junction, Vermont.

E: *Morris is the inn cat—known as the world's friendliest.*

When the stars are lost and rain seeps coldly
upon the ground, how wonderful to find a lighted inn.

The Scottish Lion
North Conway, New Hampshire
03860

Innkeepers: John & Phyllis Morris; Jack & Judy Hurley, owners.
Telephone: 603-356-2482
Rooms: Eight, five baths.
Rates: $15 per person, for bed and breakfast.
Facilities: Open all year, breakfast for house guests only, lunch, dinner, bar. Parking. Scottish Lion Import Shop, with imports from the Emerald Isles such as cut crystal, jewelry, and those hard-to-find tartans. Free catalogue available.

The rooms are cozy, one has an eyelet-trimmed canopy bed, another a spool bed with a patchwork quilt. All are charming. A hearty Scottish breakfast is served to house guests. The whole inn is full of fine ☛ Scottish paintings. Do not miss any of them.

Food, of course, features the best of Scottish touches and is rated three stars in the Mobil Guide. Highland Game Pie which is venison, beef, hare and fowl simmered in wine and baked in puff pastry may sound strange, but a gentleman spoke to me who had had it the night before. His report, "Delicious." Hot Scottish oatcakes are served instead of bread or rolls. A marvelous dish named Rumbledethumps is one of the potato choices, what a taste. I must tell you one more called Forth Lobster Lady Tweedsmuir, tender pieces of lobster in a delicate cream and Drambuie sauce, stuffed in the shell. You must try this dish.

The inn has a long list of special pleasures from the pub such as a Hoot Mon cocktail, St. Andrews Hole-in-One or Loch Ness Monster, and more and more. The desserts, Scottish Trifle or Scots Crumpets with fresh fruit and honey are but a few. They also serve a very special coffee.

The Import Shop features the finest of imports from Scotland, England and Ireland. They have over 300 different tartan ties, plus wools, cashmeres, crystal, thistle pottery and much more. Do go and enjoy.

How to get there: Take Route 16 from Conway, then Route 302 to North Conway.

E: *When you come down the road and see the magnificent flag streaming out in the wind you just can't go by. Stop for a drink, if you can't stay the night. You'll love it.*

olive Metcalf

Stonehurst Manor
North Conway, New Hampshire
03860

Innkeeper: Peter Rattay
Telephone: 603-356-3113
Rooms: 18, 12 with private bath, two suites.
Rates: $18 to $90, double occupancy, also MAP rates.
Facilities: Open all year. Breakfast, lunch, dinner, bar, meeting room for up to 50 people, brunch in summer, pool, tennis, shuffleboard, volleyball.

    This turn-of-the-century mansion is a fine country inn. Set back from the highway among stately pine trees, it makes you think you are going back in time, and in a way you are.
    The front door is huge. Once inside, you see beautiful oak wood and wonderful wall-to-wall carpet. The room to the left is all wicker and all comfort. Ahead of you is the warm living room, with walls full of ☞ books and a huge fireplace. The unusual screen and andirons were made in England. To the right of the fireplace is a 12-foot, curved window seat of another era. The lounge area has a ☞ two-seat bar, just the right size.

Relax in a high-back wicker chair in the dining room and enjoy the fine, gourmet delights of steaks, seafood, chicken, or one of the ☛ six different veal dishes served here. Desserts are just spectacular.

The staircase is a beauty, and the large rooms are beautifully appointed. ☛ Fantastic wallpapers and beautiful carpets all add to this great inn. The third floor rooms have windows at odd angles, dictated by the roof line of the house. Some rooms have porches, and one has a stained-glass door going out to its porch. There is a lot of lovely stained glass throughout the inn.

Their pool is the largest in the Mount Washington area, and is made of ☛ wood, the only wooden one I have ever seen. You swell it in the spring, just as you would a wooden boat. Cocktails are served around the pool in the summer. There are tennis courts, shuffleboard and volleyball courts. Plenty of things will keep you busy, or, like me, you might want to just sit and relax.

How to get there: The inn is on Route 16 just a short distance north of North Conway.

☛

E: *On the second floor, in one of the hall bathrooms, is a wood-enclosed steel bath tub. Quite a sight.*

olive Metcalf

Follansbee Inn
North Sutton, New Hampshire
03260

Innkeepers: Larry & Joan Wadman
Telephone: 603-927-4221
Rooms: 23, 11 with private bath.
Rates: $20 to $30, EP, double occupancy.
Facilities: Closed Monday. Restaurant closed two weeks in
    April and November. Breakfast, dinner, lounge. Skiing,
    swimming, boating.

North Sutton has an old church with an old clock that
chimes out the time. What a wonderful sound to hear. Next
door is Follansbee, and you smell great things when you
enter this fine inn.

The food at the inn is superb. ☞ All soups, breads,
salad dressings, and desserts are made right here. ☞ The
potato is baked stuffed, and it's a pleasure to get one piping
hot. There are several steaks to choose from, and hand-
breaded onion rings taste as divine as they sound. You could
try the trout, or scampi, either crab or shrimp. Add to these,
veal, prepared three different ways, chicken, and linguini.

But you haven't had it all until you try the homemade desserts.

There is much to do in the area, such as riding, golf, skiing, or just sitting in the living rooms with a book or needlework. The rooms are amply bright and comfortable. What more could one want? This is a lovely inn.

How to get there: Take I-91 north to Ascutney, Vermont. Follow Route 103 to Route 11 east, to Route 114. Proceed to North Sutton and the inn.

E: The innkeepers have traveled all over the world, and the inn reflects the treasures they accumulated.

A night at an inn adds a tinge to the coming day that cannot be described, only be enjoyed.

Philbrook Farm Inn
Shelburne, New Hampshire
03581

Innkeepers: Connie Leger and Nancy Philbrook
Telephone: 603-466-3831
Rooms: 19, six with private bath, plus five cottages with
    housekeeping arrangements.
Rates: $25 to $28.50 per person, MAP, double occupancy.
Facililies: Closed end of October to December 26, and April 1
    to May 1. Breakfast, lunch, dinner, BYOB lounge, hik-
    ing, cross-country and downhill skiing, snowshoeing,
    Ping-Pong, pool, library.

In 1861 Philbrook Farm started as an inn. Today it is still
an inn and still has Philbrooks living here, running it in fine
New England tradition. With over 1,000 acres there is plenty
of room to roam any season of the year.

This is a very peaceful and relaxed inn. ☞ The library
is comfortably crowded with good books. Fireplaces are all
over. There is even a player piano in the dining room. A
lovely Victorian living room has card tables and an old pump

organ. The TV lounge has walls of Currier & Ives prints plus a good fireplace.

Food is served here family-style and prepared from 🐖 scratch. The baked goods are made daily. Every Sunday features roast chicken, and Sunday morning fare is pure New England, with cod fish balls and corn bread. Saturday gives another New England special, namely baked beans. The gardens provide fresh vegetables and good salads, and the homemade soups are a meal in themselves.

Bedrooms are furnished with antiques, some lovely, four-poster beds, and a collection of old bowl and pitcher sets, really the best I have ever seen.

How to get there: The inn is 1½ miles off Route 2. Going north, look for a direction sign on your right, and turn right. Cross the railroad tracks and then a bridge. Turn right at the crossroads and go a half mile to the inn, which is on North Road.

E: *The playroom, with its collection of* 🐖 *old farm tools and kitchen utensils, is a nice reminder that sometimes nice things are saved.*

You cannot hide a good country inn.

Snowvillage Lodge
Snowville, New Hampshire
03849

Innkeepers: Pat & Ginger Blymyer
Telephone: 603-447-2818
Rooms: 14, 11 with private bath.
Rates: $30 to $35 per person, MAP; EP available.
Facilities: Closed October 30 to Thanksgiving and end of snow to Memorial Day. All major credit cards accepted. Tennis courts, downhill skiing, cross-country from the inn door, ski rentals and instruction, riding, canoe rides, sleigh rides, racquet ball, hiking nearby, movies and shopping.

Hollywood has lost a good lighting director and an award-winning hairdresser for the stars, but Snowvillage has won a set of better-than-average innkeepers. While Pat is rather new at being chef, he is doing everything just right. We had the best ☛ Veal Picatta ever here.

There is one main course served each night, and whatever it might be, rest assured it will be scrumptious. Tanya, one of the Blymer's daughters, is making the pastries, and epicurian talent must run in the family, because they were excellent.

The view from the inn is breathtaking. Mount Washington and the whole Presidential Range, plus the rest of the White Mountains, greet your eyes everywhere you look. In summer at the top of Foss Mountain, right at the inn, you can eat your fill of wild blueberries.

Rooms are comfortable and spacious, with tons of towels in luscious colors. The living room, with a huge fireplace and comfortable couches all around, makes this an inn to relax in. A huge porch surrounds the inn, with views that almost take your breath away.

There is a service bar and lounge, and here you can meet the four-footed members of the family. The dogs are Flump and Louise. Three cats come in four colors. Hound Dog is the gray beauty, BN (for black nose) is black and white, and Hannibal is orange all over.

For you inveterate shoppers, fear not; North Conway is but 15 or 20 minutes away.

Ginger is everywhere you need her, and just is a natural innkeeper.

How to get there: Out of Conway on Route 153, go five miles to Crystal Lake. Turn left, go about 1¼ miles, turn right at the Snowvillage sign and go up the hill, three-quarters of a mile to the inn.

E: Plants are everywhere. I have a slip from a huge cactus.

Oliva Metcalf

The Homestead
Sugar Hill, New Hampshire
03585

Innkeepers: Esther Serafini, Barbara Serafini Hayward
Telephone: 603-823-5564 or 9577
Rooms: 10 in main house, each with running water, sharing four baths. Seven rooms with private bath in the house across the street.
Rates: $35 to $45, MAP, per person.
Facilities: Closed April to mid-May, and November 1 to December 15, except for a very special Thanksgiving week. Breakfast, dinner, BYOB.

Essie Serafini is a legend in her own time. She has been at the inn for 60 years. Her first job, at the age of 10, was to pass the relish tray. The inn has just celebrated 🐿 100 years, and good friends presented Essie with a magnificent $8,000 Gulbransen electric organ. Essie does not read music and does not have to. Wow, can she play. Back 100 years her family charged $3.00 a week for room and board.

There are many original family antiques which furnish the rooms of The Homestead. One of the beds, a pine four-poster, came by ox cart from Richmond, New Hampshire. In the parlour is a handhooked rug, 9 feet by 5 feet, all about New Hampshire identifying dozens of landmarks, animals and birds. This rug was done by Essie. She also wrote a delightful booklet titled, "Tales, Tours and Taste Treats," full of folklore, on sale at the inn or next door at the Sampler, a shop run by Essie's daughter, Barbara.

The rooms are spotless, what else would you expect from this lady, and the food is superb. Essie still finds time to do most of this. She is a powerhouse of a woman.

The inn has a very special thing about Thanksgiving week. People come from all over for this special treat, but reserve early.

How to get there: Take Exit 38 from I-93 to Route 117. The Homestead is about three miles up the hill on Route 117. Or coming from the west, turn east on Route 117 from Route 302.

E: Essie is such a special, warm, wonderful person, just love her.

301

Sunset Hill House
Sugar Hill, New Hampshire
03585

Innkeepers: Betty Lou Carmichel and Douglas Reed
Telephone: 603-823-5522
Rooms: 35, 33 with private bath.
Rates: $45 to $55 single and $40 to $50 double MAP.
Facilities: Open all year. Breakfast, lunch and dinner. Bar and lounge. Nine hole golf course, putting green, paddle and regular tennis, croquet, pool, shuffleboard, cross-country ski shop, touring trails, beauty and gift shops.

The view from the inn is spectacular. You are seeing the Presidential and Franconia ranges of the White Mountains, and, as the innkeepers say, they are above the fog-line.

You can see from the list under "facilities" that there is something for everyone to do here. ☞ Children are more than welcome, (well behaved ones, of course).

There are five dining rooms, all very nicely done, along the back of the inn with incredible views of the White Mountains and the pool. The pool, by the way, is really unique, having a separate ☞ whirlpool section with a

302

waterfall down to the regular pool. Very nicely done. The inn serves lunch here in summer.

Doug is the chef with a menu that changes daily. I had veal, and I did not need a knife to cut it. Also had a cream of cauliflower soup that was excellent. Desserts, all homemade, are unusual and good. Rooms are large. The beds are very comfortable with feather pillows. How nice not to have a lump of foam under your head.

These two young people are trying very hard to succeed, and they are making it, especially with the help of two great inn dogs, Alex, a Siberbian Husky, and Chuckey who is a Malemute.

How to get there: Take Exit 38 from I-93 to Route 117. The inn is about 3 miles up the hill on Route 117 just beyond The Homestead Inn.

E: Beds turned down at night always turn me on.

olive Metcalf

Dexters
Sunapee, New Hampshire
03782

Innkeepers: Frank & Shirley Simpson
Telephone: 603-763-5571
Rooms: 17, with bath.
Rates: $35 to $45, MAP per person, double occupancy.
Facilities: Closed mid-October to mid-June. Breakfast, lunch, dinner, bar. Tennis, outdoor pool. Fresh fruit and flowers in your room, no credit cards.

Your day starts with 🖙 juice and coffee served in your room at a time you set the night before. Or you can try being really spoiled and have your complete breakfast served in bed, but you will miss the lovely, morning view of Lake Sunapee from the dining room.

The lounge and bar are unique, with games, books, and even a little shop just outside the door. The rooms at the inn are a bit above average, with some carefully thought-out, unusual, wallpapers. 🖙 The pillows are made of heavenly feathers, and I mean plenty of them. Most of the beds are antiques that came down through the Simpson family.

The feature of the inn is tennis, and if you are a buff you will love it, for there are three fine courts. And after a game there is a large outdoor pool to cool off in.

And for a good summer or fall activity there are some of the loveliest walking and hiking trails right on the inn property.

There is a special recreation room in the barn for all ages, but it is keyed to those under 16 who need a place of their own when the five o'clock cocktail hour begins.

How to get there: Take I-89 out of Concord and follow Exit 12 to Route 11, to 103B at Sunapee. Or take I-91 out of Springfield and follow Exit 8 to Claremont, New Hampshire, to Route 103. The turn to the inn is marked by a sign 200 yards south of the intersection of 103 and 11. The inn is about 1½ miles off Route 103.

C

E: *Frank is one of our special innkeepers, right on top of everything.*

olive Metcalf

The Playhouse Inn
Whitefield, New Hampshire
03598

Innkeepers: Lucienne and Noel Lacan
Telephone: 603-837-2527
Rooms: 12, eight with private bath.
Rates: $18 to $34 double occupancy, EP.
Facilities: Closed October 15 to May 10, and Mondays in
spring and fall. Open every day in July and August.
Breakfast and lunch in summer, dinner. Beer Garden,
cocktail lounge and cabaret show in July and August,
summer stock theater, swimming pool, golf and tennis
five minutes away.

With the Weathervane Theater just across the lawn,
Lucienne and Noel Lacan have taken the playhouse theme
for their delightful country inn. Noel is the chef, and the
menu, from Prelude through Curtain Calls, proves it in every
scene and act. There are those who hate vegetables, and then
there's me. Endives Meuniere, Braised Heart of Celery, Lima
Bean Bretonne, Mushrooms Sauteed Provencale . . . who
needs meat?

The new swimming pool, with its view of the mountains, is lovely. There are six fireplaces in this comfortable old house. ☞ From the Backstage Bar to the Limelighter Restaurant, the theatrical touch is here, but with a really solid Gallic accent.

☞ Be sure to catch the enthralling caberet held six nights a week in the Backstage Lounge. Five bouncingly talented youngsters—none are over 30—raise the rafters with song and merriment and bring a tear to more than one eye. Each evening offers an entirely different show, so feel free to go twice, or three times or more.

How to get there: Take I-93, then Route 3 into Whitefield. The inn is in the center of town.

E: *The menu is great! Snails en Surprise have a new approach, and to finish off with Flaming Spanish coffee is indeed a switch.*

An unlit hearth in a good tavern is warmer by equators than a blazing fire where there is no love.

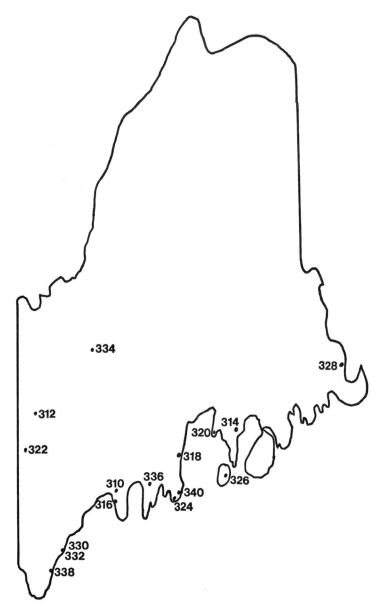

•334

328•

•312

•322

314
320
•318

336
310
316
324 340
326

330
332
338

numbers on map refer to page numbers in this book

Maine

Olive Metcalf

Grane's Fairhaven Inn
Bath, Maine
04530

Innkeepers: Jane Wyllie and Gretchen Williams
Telephone: 207-443-4391
Rooms: Nine, four shared baths.
Rates: $20 to $32, double occupancy.
Facilities: Open all year. Breakfast. BYOB lounge. Fireplaces, cross-country skiing, snowshoeing. Special packages for weekends and major holidays. Breakfast is extra.

"Truth is never pure and rarely simple. Better to wear out than to rust out. Remember my friend, all things must end." These are a few of the needlepoint sayings on the ☛ 14 steps going up the back stairs of this lovely old inn. The ingenious rug was done by a former owner and the top step is "Knowledge Grows by Steps." Only in a country inn will you find things like this.

Rooms at Grane's are neat and very clean, with antiques, good beds, and wonderful views. The front of the inn looks out on a salt tidal cove of the Kennebec River.

Breakfast is a thing of joy, with ☛ fresh fruit and

310

souffles. I can still taste the hot bran muffins, and to top them off, the girls make their own jams and jellies. All this good eating is served in two lovely dining rooms.

The Tavern Library is a BYOB bar with fireplace, good chairs, and lots of fun. The English Bishop is a dandy hot drink for cold skiers. It is composed of port wine, oranges, cloves, honey, and brandy. If you have a cold it is just what the doctor, or a kindly bartender, ordered.

How to get there: On Route 1, just short of Bath, take the exit marked New Meadows. Go north a half mile until the road dead ends. Take a right, and an immediate left on Whiskeag Road. One-and-one-half miles beyond is North Bath Road. Take a left here, and the inn is on your left in about a half mile.

E: *I have two cats, one Himalayan and one Maine Coon. At the inn is one Maine Coon, Cleo, and one bluepoint called Tuptim.*

When life dwindles thin and you wonder
if the sun will rise on another day,
seek perhaps an unfamiliar but rejuvenating bed
in a nearby country inn.

The Bethel Inn
Bethel, Maine
04217

Innkeeper: Dick Rasor; Mr. Diebel, manager.
Telephone: 207-824-2175
Rooms: 65, all with private bath.
Rates: $33 to $53, MAP, per person.
Facilities: Open all year. Breakfast, lunch, dinner, bar. Golf,
tennis, swimming, cross-country skiing from the door,
down-hill nearby, sauna, fireplaces, indoor games. The
inn has its own walking tour guide book.

The Bethel Inn faces the village common of Bethel,
which is a National Historic District complete with beautifully restored churches, public buildings, and private homes.
The rear of the inn overlooks its own 85 acres, and beyond to
the White Mountains.

Guest rooms have private baths and direct dial telephones. ☛ All are individually decorated. Hilda Donahue
has been the housekeeper for 35 years. She should win a
medal for the way she keeps the inn.

The huge living room, music room, library, and dining

rooms are for the comfort of the guests. New this past year was the screening in of the long back porch, which overlooks the inn golf course. What a ☞ perfect place for summer dining.

Downstairs at the Bethel Inn is another world, and a fine one, with live music playing anything from Glenn Miller to Bach. A nice barroom that serves a light supper menu until midnight is an added touch for the late skier or walker. And in winter you can have hot cider, hot buttered rum, and ☞ Glogg. I had several Gloggs to help me fight a nagging cold. Nice remedy.

Dick is starting his own yard sale to be held the first weekend in November. It starts with things from the inn, but anyone can bring whatever he wishes to sell. An annual affair, we think it will be Maine's largest tag sale. And largest or not, it should be a whale of a lot of fun.

Skiing is super up here, with Sunday River and Mount Abram right at hand. ☞ The inn has special ski package weekends, so if this is your bag, do check on them.

How to get there: Bethel is located at the intersection of U.S. Route 2 and Maine Routes 5, 26, and 35. From the south, take Exit 11 off the Maine Turnpike at Gray, and follow Route 26 to Bethel. The inn is on the green.

E: ☞ *The service plates in the dining room are Syracuse china, and all are hand painted. Each of the 100 plates has its individual pattern.*

olive Metcalf

Blue Hill Inn
Blue Hill, Maine
04614

Innkeepers: Jean & Fred Wakelin
Telephone: 207-374-2844
Rooms: Nine doubles, with bath.
Rates: $36 per room for two, $30 single.
Facilities: Open all year. Breakfast and dinner. And just about
    everything you can do on the great coast of Maine.

Harry is a big, beautiful black Lab who greets all people at the inn. This sort of tells you what to expect at this friendly place, built in 1840. The rooms are impressive, with queen and king-size beds so a tired body has enough room to really relax. The living and sitting rooms are comfortably furnished with a nook for set-ups, as this is a bring-your-own- bottle inn.

Jean does the cooking in an ample country kitchen, and Fred is everywhere. He came down out of a tree he was pruning to greet me when I arrived unannounced.

The Blue Hill Country Club offers golf, tennis, and swimming. The Kneisel Music School has concerts, and there is cross-country skiing in winter. This is a lovely town and a most scenic area just to browse in.

How to get there: From Route 1 in Bucksport, take Route 15 right into Blue Hill.

E: This whole area is taking my breath away.

In the autumn, especially as one ages,
a firelit tavern in an excellent inn cannot be bettered
by the smallest mansions in Christendom.

Olive Metcalf

The Stowe House
Brunswick, Maine
04011

Innkeepers: Peg and Bob Mathews
Telephone: 207-725-5543
Rooms: 55, all with private bath.
Rates: $32.50 to $45.
Facilities: Open all year. Breakfast, lunch and dinner. Continental breakfast off season (November 1 to May 1). TV and telephones in the rooms. Gift shop, bar, theatre. Accessible to wheelchairs.

Harriet Beecher Stowe wrote *Uncle Tom's Cabin* while she lived here. Longfellow and Hawthorne stayed here while attending Bowdoin College in the 1820's. Plenty of history is within these walls.

There is a potbellied stove in the lobby and another in the living room. Nautical memorabilia abound, some on loan from the Bath Marine Museum. ☛ The ship model outside the pub is of the famous *Corsair*. Maine's seafaring history is also highlighted in the Taproom, an elegant pub where, surrounded by nautical antiques, you can enjoy a quiet cocktail before dinner.

The rooms are very modern, even including color televisions. Extra conveniences and personalized service add a new dimension to this unique, historic inn.

Shopping is right at hand in the inn with Stowe-Away, a shop that has everything from Christmas goodies to original needlepoint designs and gourmet cookware. There is a good section on New England handicrafts.

Maine lobster is, of course, available here along with many other special treats. To name one, there is Filet of Sole Saint Croix, a delicately broiled filet of sole with asparagus and mushrooms in a lobster sauce. The standard dishes of steak, chicken or veal are all a bit differently prepared.

In summer there is a cabaret theater on the second floor with professional casts. This is a nice touch to a country inn.

How to get there: Go north on Route 1 to Brunswick. Go straight on Pleasant Street, and turn right on Maine Street, then left on Cleveland at the church, and then left on Federal.

ጠ

E: Topsy, a black poodle, is the inn dog. He shares his duties with Widget, a great cat.

Olive Metcalf

Camden Harbor Inn
Camden, Maine
04843

Innkeepers: Jim and Laureen Gilbert
Telephone: 207-236-4200
Rooms: 17, nine private baths.
Rates: $35 to $52, double occupancy, EPB.
Facilities: Open all year. Breakfast, dinner. TV in lounge, golf
    nearby, skiing, sailing, and Camden Harbor, a delight in
    itself.

Camden Harbor is one of the best-known ports in
Maine, and one of the prettiest. Boats of yesteryear, both sail
and power, as well as beautiful yachts of today, moor here by
the rolling mountains that come right down to rocky shores.
The inn sits up high above all of this and affords you a
☛ panoramic view all year-round.
    The rooms are rather small, but neat as a pin. The dining
room has a fireplace and a very warm atmosphere. With the
dining room is the ☛ Thirsty Whale Tavern, and no better
spot for a touch or two, especially with the sounds of weekend folk music.

Jim has recently enclosed the porch overlooking Penobscot Bay and the mountains with ceiling-high casement windows, to make a second dining room with a spectacular view.

There are walking tours, bicycle trips, and nature walks in and around Camden. There is hardly a spot in this whole lovely Maine town that is not worth a visit. In July the Penobscot Folk Festival draws crowds to the Rockport Opera House.

This is a wonderful town to muddle about in for days.

How to get there: From Route 1, which runs through the center of town, turn up Bayview Street to #83.

E: *Andre, the famous seal, lives in Rockport Harbor all summer. He winters at the aquarium in Boston and for 16 years has been swimming back on his own. Go see him. You will love him.*

Come back 100 years and stay at my inn.

The Pentagöet Inn
Castine, Maine
04421

Innkeeper: Natalie F. Saunders
Telephone: 207-326-8616
Rooms: 14, three with private baths, two with ½ baths.
Rates: $26 to $36 double occupancy EP.
Facilities: Open all year. Breakfast, dinner, Sunday brunch. Bar and lounge. Maine's most extensive wine list says the owner.

The Pentagöet is a lovely inn located on the unspoiled coast of beautiful Penobscot Bay. Built in 1894 this Victorian inn offers the traveler warmth and a very friendly atmosphere.

The living room holds many of Natalie's plants, has a wood burning stove and comfortable places to just relax. The dining room serves breakfast and dinner. The chef prepares one entree each evening. ☛ It is served in five courses. Seating is limited in order for you to enjoy the very best in dining.

The bedrooms are restful, some of them with little

alcoves with windows that allow you a view of the town and harbor. All in all a very nice part of the world to be in.

There is good Maine fishing, sailing and power boating, a nine hole golf course and dozens of islands nearby for delightful picnicking or just exploring. The Maine Maritime Academy is here in Castine, and their training ship, State of Maine, is open to the public.

Bear, a Maine coon cat, and Spot, a black and white general breed, help run the inn. They really are in charge.

How to get there: Take Route 95 from Portland to the "Coastal Region—Brunswick, Bath, Route 1" Exit. Follow Route 1 to Bucksport and two miles beyond turn right onto Route 175. Take Route 175 to Route 166, which takes you into Castine.

E: *The* 👉 *porch that overlooks the town and harbor and serves lunch and tea, and sometimes dinner, is my spot in summer.*

Trifles make an inn, but an inn is no trifle.

Center Lovell Inn
Center Lovell, Maine
04016

Innkeepers: Bil and Sue Mosca
Telephone: 207-925-1575
Rooms: Five, two with private bath.
Rates: $61 to $84 MAP, double occupancy.
Facilities: Closed March 15 to May 15, and October 15 to December 15. Breakfast is for guests only. Box lunches available, dinner, service bar, swimming in Kezar Lake, cross-country skiing from the inn, downhill skiing nearby.

Overlooking Kezar Lake in Center Lovell is a fine, gourmet country inn. People come from all over to sample Bil's food, and no wonder. He features northern Italian cuisine at its best. Veal marsala, veal margarita or veal parmigiano alforno are excellent and unusual. ☛ Pollo ala Nicolo Firenze is boneless chicken with a different stuffing, baked and basted with honey butter. And do try the shrimp or Maine lobster. The pasta dishes are spectacular, but the house specialty is ☛ lobster Fra Diavola di Center Lovell

Inn. Two days' reservation notice for this gem is worth it. Topping it all off is fresh, rich, Italian cheesecake.

The recipes used here have been passed down through five traceable generations of Moscas and require the finest ingredients that money and knowledge can obtain. This is why Bil drives to Boston's North End every week. All of this fine food is served in a small, homey and unpretentious dining room in front of a huge fireplace.

The front parlor has an almost original 🐄 Hammond electric organ still in fine tune and a challenge to play. Here, too, is an 1870 fire box that my publisher fell in love with.

The porch goes around three sides of the inn. It overlooks the lake and in the summer you can dine out here. There are five downhill ski areas within half an hour, and you can cross-country from the back door. A beauty of a Labrador guards the inn. His name is Sabbetino. The area also offers fishing, canoeing, hiking and the annual Fryeburg Fair in October.

How to get there: Coming either way on Route 302, turn north at Fryeburg, Maine onto Route 5. Fourteen miles north, the lake will appear on your left, and the inn on your right.

E: 🐄 *Three times a year, New Year's, Memorial Day and Columbus Day, the Mosca's set aside three days for gourmandizing. From Friday through Sunday you eat and forget diet.*

The Craignair Inn
Clark Island, Maine
04859

Innkeepers: Norman and Terry Smith
Telephone: 207-594-7644
Rooms: 20, with shared baths.
Rates: $25 to $33, MAP, per person.
Facilities: Open all year. Breakfast, dinner for six or more in winter, BYOB. Special diets furnished upon reasonable notice.

This isn't a fancy inn, but it is comfortable. It was built about 50 years ago as a boarding house for quarry workers. It is hung on the edge of the water, with rocks, tidal flats, an ocean inlet, and loads of peace and quiet. The quarry has long since been worked out, but you can swim there in the saltwater that rises and falls with the tide. If you worry about old wooden buildings, sleep relaxed here.

There is always something to do at Craignair. If the fog rolls in, cozy up to the fire in the sitting room. When it snows, the Camden Snow Bowl Ski Area is a short drive away. Nearby towns and villages offer diversified activity stops, including antiques shops, art galleries, museums, and specialty shops. Or you could attend a concert, golf, play tennis, ride horseback, bicycle, sail, or catch one of the numerous ☛ festivals paying homage to seafood, blueberries, chicken, sailboats, and history.

If tidal pools, clam flats, islands, meadows, and spruce forests invite you, come to Craignair in any season.

How to get there: Go to Thomaston on Route 1, then take Route 131 south for about six miles, and turn left on Route 73 for about a mile to Clark Island Road. Take a right, and the inn is at the end of the road.

E: *No excuse now, if you are a weight watcher, or on a salt-free diet.* ☛ *Terry will stick to your diet if you let her know a day or two ahead of time. There's one entree only each evening, but what variety. And on Saturday, enjoy that traditional Maine dinner, fresh lobster with steamers.*

Having had an excellent meal and a lovely evening,
I tucked myself in bed knowing I had sinned
but it did not seem to matter.

Pilgrims Inn
Deer Isle, Maine
04627

Innkeepers: George & Eleanor Pavloff
Telephone: 207-348-6615
Rooms: 10, six with bath.
Rates: $300 MAP, per person per week; $48 daily.
Facilities: Closed from late October to late May. Swimming, sailing, bicycling, clamming, golf and tennis at the Island Club.

You are welcomed by the glowing hearths of the many fireplaces throughout this rambling inn. The paneled parlor and dining room overlook Northwest Harbour, little changed from 100 or more years ago. In the words of the inn's brochure, ☞ "The bedrooms all face the water, Northwest Harbour or the mill pond, either one so easy to look at."

This was Squire Haskell's home. He built his sawmill on the pond. An industrious citizen, he also helped frame the Maine Constitution back in 1793.

George Pavloff is all about and handles the cocktail

hour in the great common room at six o'clock every evening. The fireplace down here is better than 10 feet wide and is surrounded with comfortable couches and chairs. The room is full of books and games for all to enjoy.

Elli does the cooking and very well, thank you. We were served turkey done Elli's way one evening, and a subtle lamb roast another time. Both were superb. The way dinner is served is a particular pleasure. A local potter, Charles Hance, has made all the stonewear utensils that Elli uses to serve each table family-style. In the summer there is a barn attached to the inn which has been made into a most attractive dining room overlooking the mill pond.

Swim at the causeway by the inn or sail in the best sailing waters in America. Take a mail boat to a nearby island, fish, antique, have a picnic, hear chamber music concerts at the Kneisel Hall summer school in Blue Hill, or just sit and talk to the two inn dogs, both champion springer spaniels.

The Pavloffs recently have taken over the management of the nearby Goose Cove Lodge, which has 70 acres and a half mile of gorgeous ocean frontage. Here there are cottages and a central dining room. Open from June 15 to September 15, rates run from $200 to $260 per person, per week, MAP.

How to get there: From Route 1 turn right after Bucksport on Route 15, which goes right to Deer Isle. In the village turn right on Main Street, and the inn is immediately on your left.

E: *In the off season the seven o'clock dinner hour may be moved ahead, but who cares when it is so good.*

olive Metcalf

Lincoln House Country Inn
Dennysville, Maine
04628

Innkeepers: Mary Carol and Gerald Haggerty
Telephone: 207-726-3953
Rooms: Six, four baths, all semi-private, five working fire-
places, four wood stoves.
Rates: $20 to $25 single and $35 to $40 double occupancy.
Facilities: Open all year. Closed Mondays for food. Breakfast
for house guests, dinner by reservation. November 1 to
end of May dinner is served only Fridays and Saturdays.
Full bar. Good wine list.

When you walk in the side door of the inn you are in
what once was the summer kitchen and now is a library full
of books with a huge fireplace hung with old cooking equipment and one Japanese wok! On through Mary Carol's
kitchen you find two delightful dining rooms. Beyond is a
large living room with a baby grand piano. This is an inn you
can feel totally at home in.
Mary Carol's kitchen really turns out exceptional food,
best 🐑 lamb I ever had. It was prepared quite differently

and only Mary Carol can tell you how. Her breakfast muffins almost out-do her lamb.

The inn is a handsome yellow four-square Georgian Colonial perched above the Denny River, one of the few rivers where you can find the Atlantic salmon. John Audubon once stayed here, and was so impressed he named the "Lincoln Sparrow" for his hosts. The inn was built by an ancester of President Lincoln in 1787.

Jerry is a master restorer and perfectionist. It shows all over the inn. The woodshed, a village pub, has a bar that Jerry carved from a 4,000 pound elm trunk with a bear's head carved at one end. The woodshed has fun on Thursday nights in the winter. It is "open mike" time and all local amateurs come and do their thing. Sundays it is international dart shoots with neighboring Canada. The U.S. seems to always win and whether this is their ability or Jerry's liberal beers we do not know.

You will love this inn, but it is a long way off, so do make reservations ahead.

How to get there: Route 1 goes right by Dennysville. Driving up take the second sign into Dennysville, just after you have crossed the Denny River. Turn left and you will find the inn almost immediately on your right.

E: ☛ *Bald eagles and osprey are seen here, and families of seals swim in the river. It is a long way up here but worth every mile.*

Captain Lord Mansion
Kennebunkport, Maine
04046

Innkeepers: Beverly Davis & Rick Litchfield
Telephone: 207-967-3141
Rooms: 15 with private bath, 10 with working fireplaces.
Rates: $49 to $69, double, including tax and breakfast.
Facilities: Open all year. Breakfast only. There are many places to explore here, such as Perkins Cove and the Rachel Carson Wildlife Refuge. The inn itself will take time to see. Not an inn for children.

We keep looking for a word to do justice to describing this inn. Exquisite is not enough. Some of the 🖙 oriental rugs are from mainland China, with colors that are unbelievable. One of the beds is a four-poster 12 feet high. Rugs and wallpaper, thanks to Beverly's eye, are well coordinated, 🖙 thirsty towels are abundant, and extra blankets and pillows help make your stay better than pleasant.

🖙 Ten of the guest rooms have working fireplaces. There are 12 throughout the inn. Most of the rooms have padded, deep, window seats, a great place to relax and day-dream.

Throughout the inn are portraits of past owners in the Lord family. There is still much of the original Lord furniture. A handsome dining room table with carved feet and chairs belonged to Nathaniel Lord's grandson, Charles Clark, and is dated 1880. The wallpaper in one bedroom that is still beautifully intact dates also from 1880. The paper in the front parlor goes back to 1812.

Breakfast is the only meal served, and it is a rare treat. You eat at a huge table in the center of a kitchen that has about as big a wood stove as we have seen. For other meals there are many fine restaurants in Kennebunkport.

This is a bring-your-own-bottle inn, but from the scenic cupola on its top to the parlours on the first floor, you will find many great places to enjoy a drink.

How to get there: From I-95, take Exit 3 to Kennebunkport and Route 35 to the port. From Route 1 take Route 9 into Dock Square. Turn right on Ocean Avenue. Go 3/10 of a mile, and then turn left at River Green.

E: Rick knows the history of the house and loves to tell it as it was, so do ask him.

Village Cove Inn
Kennebunkport, Maine
04046

Innkeepers: Jacques and Carol Gagnon
Telephone: 207-967-3993
Rooms: Five, one with private bath, 30 rooms in annex plus one cottage, all with private bath.
Rates: EP $46 to $55, double occupancy.
Facilities: Open all year, breakfast, lunch, dinner, TV, bar, inside and outside pools. Sunday brunch in winter.

The Village Cove Inn nestles in the trees on the hillside overlooking Chick's Cove, just a few minutes from Dock Square. I must say one thing for Maine, and that is its tides really go out, way out. Quite a sight to see.

The outside pool is right at your door, a real nice place to just relax and enjoy. ☛ The inside pool is solar-heated. In winter the large function room by the pool will become ☛ an exercise room, a unique feature for a country inn.

The Inn staff conducts art workshops from May through October at both of its inns, Thorn Hill Lodge in Jackson, New Hampshire, and here. Write for their mountain and sea vacation package. Water colors, oils, drawing, and pastels will be taught.

The Port Pub is where it's happening, with food at its best whether it's breakfast or lunch, with a huge selection of soups, sandwiches and ☛ very special salads. Dinner features lobster prepared three different ways, scallops and other fish dishes. Duck is excellent, as is the veal. The salad bar is different because it is both a salad and a wine bar. I was at the inn for the wine tasting for choosing the wines that will be served, all nice and all dry.

Children have their ☛ own menu with names like Batman & Robin, The Scooby-do, or The Pink Panther. This is a nice touch for the kids.

The Ledge Room and Lounge, carved right into "the rockbound coast of Maine," is a neat place for a good drink.

How to get there: From Kennebunk follow Route 9 or 9-A into Kennebunkport where the two roads join. Continue on Route 9 until it turns right at Main Street. Stay on Main Street after Route 9 leaves you on the left. Bear right at the fork, and the inn is three-quarters of a mile along on your right.

E: *The spiral staircase goes from the restaurant around down to the bar. It is a nice trip.*

Winter's Inn
Kingfield, Maine
04947

Innkeeper: Michael Thom; Esther Thompson, manager.
Telephone: 207-265-5421
Rooms: 11, four with private bath.
Rates: $42 to $48 per person MAP. Ask for special family and
group rates.
Facilities: Closed in May and June. Breakfast and dinner.
Dining room, fireside cocktail lounges, intimate bar.
Tennis, swimming pool, cross-country skiing from the
door, bus service to Sugarloaf Mountain and from
nearby airports upon request.

Located in the heart of the western Maine mountains,
inbetween Bigelow, Sugarloaf, and Saddleback, sits Winter's
Inn on top of a ten-acre hill on the edge of town. It is a
restored neo-Georgian manor house, built at the turn of the
century for Amos Greene Winter. The house had fallen into
sad disrepair until it was rescued in 1972 by Michael Thom, a
young architect from Cambridge, Massachusetts, and To-
ronto, Canada. ☛ Much to his pride, the building has now

been listed on the National Register of Historic Places.

Elegant without being stiff or pretentious, the inn has been decorated with ☞ handsome wallpapers. The walls are hung with a fine collection of oil paintings and gold-framed mirrors. The view from the dining room windows of the western mountains is breathtaking. The view is the same from the swimming pool.

☞ Food served in Le Papillon is delightful, a continuing surprise in this faraway inn at the back of beyond. Guests can spend their days climbing mountains, come home to the inn for a swim and a drink, then dress for dinner and dine elegantly, savoring the best of both worlds.

Hunting, fishing, hiking along the Appalachian Trail, and canoeing welcome outdoors people. Downhill skiers are especially happy here, but so is the lady guest ensconced by the pool with her needlepoint or book.

Balthazar's Pub features backgammon, light jazz and light classical music, onion soup, quiche du jour, and Sicilian pizza.

How to get there: Take the Maine Turnpike to Exit 12, continue on Route 4 to Farmington, and then on Route 27 to Kingfield. Kingfield is midway between Montreal and Quebec City, on the way to the Maine coast or enroute to the Maritimes. The inn is on a rise near the center of town.

E: *There lives here an inn cat, Balthazar. He is orange and white and as regal as his name. Once I had a look-alike cat, Alleycat, just as majestic.*

The Newcastle Inn
Newcastle, Maine
04553

Innkeepers: George and Sandra Thomas
Telephone: 207-563-5685
Rooms: 20, nine with private bath.
Rates: From $17 with semi-private bath and some $24 with
    private bath, double occupancy.
Facilities: Open all year. Breakfast only, at the moment, but
    dinner will come shortly. TV in sitting room. Antique
    shop in basement.

Found on each bed here at the inn is this greeting,
"We bid you warm welcome as you enter this room. It
may not be our good fortune to come to know you this trip,
but we want you to feel this is your home while away, and
that we are eager for your comfort and happiness while our
guest. May you rest well. May you be healthy under this
roof. May your stay fulfill your every expectation. May God
bless and prosper you."

The lovely porch full of wicker furniture is always
cool in summer and is a nice way to enter this charming inn.

Breakfast is the only meal being served now, but what a breakfast, best french toast I have ever found. The dining room is charming. There is a large, comfortable living room with fireplace and another room for TV viewing.

Rooms here are Maine-size small, but are well done with white bedspreads, white curtains and clean, clean, clean.

At the inn you are within walking distance of the lovely town of Damariscotta and its salt-water tidal river. You are also within short driving distance of the famous Pemaquid peninsula with its lighthouse, fort, and beach. In the other direction you are not far from Boothbay Harbor. Do come up and enjoy this distinctive part of Maine.

How to get there: Take Route 1 to the Damariscotta exit. Turn right and turn another sharp right. The inn is on old Route 1 on the left side of the road.

E: *Good cross-country skiing is all around you, so do come up.*

olive Metcalf

The Old Village Inn
Ogunquit, Maine
03907

Innkeepers: Frederick L. Thomas and Alf B. Kristiansen
Telephone: 207-646-7088
Rooms: Six suites, one double, all with private bath.
Rates: $22 to $55 EP, double occupancy.
Facilities: Closed January and February. Dining room is closed Mondays through the winter. Ogunquit Room is available for private parties up to 20. Continental breakfast for inn guests. Lunch, dinner and a fine bar.

Fred Thomas and Alf Kristiansen have a good in-town inn that has a history going back to 1833. Interestingly, part of its history was the August 2, 1942 issue of the 🖝 *Saturday Evening Post,* which had for its cover a picture of the inn done by John Falter.

The inn is always being updated, and now there are two suites available. One of the bedrooms has a headboard made from four ladder-back chairs. According to Fred it is the only one of its kind. He should know, because he built it.

The bar is 🖝 a real, English country pub with hanging

stemware glasses, small tables, and a cooking unit off to one side. The dining rooms are different and comfortable. One is enclosed in a greenhouse, with a view of the ocean and with greenery everywhere. The Bird & Bottle is another dining room, and the newest is ☛ the enclosed porch that wraps around the front of the inn.

The Ogunquit Room is a perfect spot for a private party of up to 20 people. There is a living room with a TV, nice for the younger set, and also a room with piano and game tables.

Hard on the rock-bound coast of Maine, this inn has interests for all. The famous Ogunquit Playhouse is here, as is the newer off-Broadway repertory theater. There is plenty of fishing and swimming, and two unusual walking trails.

The Marginal Way winds you along the spectacular bay and sea, and the Trolley Trail follows an abandoned line through the woods. I have never gone by, or even near, Ogunquit without a stop at this good inn.

How to get there: The inn is at 30 Main Street in the middle of Ogunquit. Main Street is Route 1.

⚓

E: *The greenhouse is so nice. I have one at home, so I know.*

Olive Metcalf

The East Wind Inn
Tenants Harbor, Maine
04860

Innkeepers: Tim Watts and Ginny Wheeler
Telephone: 207-372-8800
Rooms: 16, six baths, one suite with private bath.
Rates: $28 to $34, EP.
Facilities: Open seven days a week, all year. Breakfast, lunch, dinner, service bar. Telephones in rooms. Deep-water anchorage for boats.

Have you dreamed of a place that has not changed in 85 years, where you can let the children roam around the town, fish off the wharf, watch fishermen unload their gear? Then load up the bicycles and head for Tenants Harbor and the East Wind Inn. Tim Watts, the innkeeper who restored this gem, has lived nearby most of his young life, watched the old white frame house deteriorate, and dreamed of restoring it so others could share the charm of "The Country of the Pointed Firs."

This inn, open every day all year, is one of the few where 🖐 you can arrive by boat and find all the charts, gasoline, and diesel fuel you need right next door.

The inn is within walking distance of the village, where you will find a library, shops, post office, and even church suppers, on a weekend. Bicycle around the Saint George peninsula, find beaches, rock cliffs, tidal pools, and old cemeteries. Or go down to Port Clyde, a real Maine fishing village, and take the ferry to Monhegan Island. In winter you can ski at the Camden Snow Bowl, a respite from other crowded slopes.

The inn itself, built in 1890, had stood vacant for more than 20 years when Tim persuaded the owner to sell it to him. And it was a good sale, for Tim has fully and lovingly restored the entire place. Hearty, home-cooked New England vittles are served three times a day in the spick-and-span dining room, with its glorious view of the harbor.

The Swiss chocolate pie is sinfully good.

How to get there: From Route 1, just east of Thomaston, take Route 131 south 9.5 miles to Tenants Harbor. Turn left at the post office and continue straight to the inn.

E: *The freshest of seafood is always available at the inn, and if you want some packed in ice to carry home with you, step next door to the Cod End Fish Market.*

And a Special Exception for Maine . . .

Throughout this guidebook I have listed only inns that are open all year, or at least most of the year. But in Maine, with its uniquely winter climate, I was presented with a problem. There are many charming inns . . . true inns . . . that just cannot stay open all year.

As an example, I ran across one lady who was still smiling bravely, out on one of those fingers of land that stick into the sea, though she had opened her inn the first of May and saw her first guest only on the first of July.

SO . . . here are some briefer descriptions of inns I like that are certainly worth visiting, when they are open.

AND . . . if I have missed a Maine inn that does stay open all year, as well I might have, I will rectify it in my next edition.

Black Point Inn, Prout's Neck, Maine 04070. Innkeeper: Normand H. Dugas. Telephone: 207-883-9468. 80 rooms, with private bath. Open from end of June until after Labor Day. Breakfast, lunch, dinner, bar. TV, elevator, parking. Leave the Maine Turnpike at Exit 7. Go east to Route 1. Turn right on Route 1, go south 2.7 miles to Route 207. Turn left on Route 207 and go five miles to the inn. Or fly Delta Airlines to Portland, 11 miles from the inn. The inn car will meet guests upon advance notice for a nominal charge. One of the most delightful, best managed, beautiful places in the state, Black Point is open such a short season. Go. ☛ The poolside luncheon, with pleasant *live* music is one of the most imaginative, delicious buffets I have encountered anywhere in my travels. The serene, spacious dining room, the welcoming living room, and lovely bedrooms are just the bare bones of this garden spot.

The Claremont, Southwest Harbor, Maine 04679. Innkeeper: John Madeira, Jr. Telephone: 207-846-5387. Thirty rooms, eight cottages, all but three suites have private baths. Open from June 15 to September 15. Breakfast, dinner, bar, marina. Accessible to wheelchairs. Tennis. Fireplaces. This is a really old-time summer place, with a beautiful new dining room that has a fabulous view of the only fjord in North America. This is a family-oriented inn, and Jay, the new innkeeper, has been coming here since he was a child. The food is genuine New England, home-baked goodies and home-grown vegetables abound. ☛ The bar is in the boat-house and couldn't be nicer.

Coveside Inn, Christmas Cove, Maine 04542. Innkeepers: Barbara & Mike Mitchell. Telephone: 207-644-8282. 18 rooms, 18 baths. Bar, restaurant, gift shop, marina. Breakfast, lunch, dinner. Open in summer only. The view from the inn is directly over the famed Christmas Cove. The Wawenock Country Club is close by and provides a well-groomed, nine-hole course. Swimmers go to Pemaquid Beach. There is much to see here, so do come and enjoy. The inn dogs, both black Labs, are Holly and Noel. ☛ This is a great place to come to by boat, with a fine harbor, spectacular views.

Dockside Guest Quarters, York, Maine 03909. Innkeepers: David and Harriette Lusty. Telephone: 207-363-2868. Open from Memorial Day through Columbus Day. Nineteen units, including some cottages, country twins that share a bath, some studies. Parking. Moorings. Breakfast, lunch and dinner except on Monday. No bar, but they have a liquor license. Come by land or sea, but come. This is the sort of place my mother was always hunting for while cruising. You know, a place where she could get off that boat. The accommodations are varied, but all are comfortable and clean. If you obey the rules, your pet is welcome. The view of the harbor is something else, and the Dockside Dining Room is turning out meals three times a day. York is a lovely little town, with lots of old buildings, and many shops.

English Meadows Inn, Kennebunkport, Maine 04046. Innkeepers: Gene and Helen Kelly. Telephone: 207-967-5766. Open early spring to late fall. Twelve rooms with continental breakfast. From the Maine Turnpike take Exit 3, turn left onto Route 35. The inn is five miles farther on your right. English Meadows is a lovely Victorian building, circa 1840. Whether you stay in the main house with brass beds, hooked and rag rugs, and other antiques, or in the panelled annex with large, fireplaced meeting rooms, you are sure to feel at home. The inn is situated on six acres of meadow and pine groves. It is just a few moments walk to Dock Square where you will find fine restaurants, shops, churches, and galleries. This has been an inn for more than 80 years.

Homewood Inn, Yarmouth, Maine 04096. Innkeepers: Fred and Colleen Webster. Telephone: 207-846-3351. 23 rooms in five houses, 11 cottages, all with private bath. 19 units with kitchens, 15 fireplaces. Weekly housekeeping rates and European Plan. Open mid-June to mid-October. Leave the Maine Turnpike at Exit 9 and go to Route 1 north. Turn right at Tuttle Road to Route 88. Turn left, and follow the signs to Homewood. This lovely old homestead has opened wide its arms with a scatter of cottages, so that more people can enjoy the many pleasures of Casco Bay. The inn is only two miles from Yarmouth, a picturesque coastal village with churches, shops, and historic attractions. Borrow a bicycle built for two and peddle along country roads. ☛ Moor your boat at the inn, and stay until you get your land legs back.

Ledgelawn Inn, Bar Harbor, Maine 04609. Innkeepers: Michael and Mary Miles. Telephone: 207-288-4596. Seventeen rooms, eight with private baths, nine fireplaces. Laundromat. Open from memorial Day to November 1. Breakfast only. BYOB. The inn is located at 66 Mountain Desert Street, close to the center of town. If you arrive in town by ferry or plane, inn personnel will pick you up. The inn, built in 1904, is one of the few "summer cottages" that survived the Great Fire of 1947. Many of the original furnishings are still here, and restoration is underway. Ask to see the ☛ Mistress' bedroom, and go up to the widow's walk for a look around. Guests here can use the tennis courts and pool at the Bar Harbor Club for a small daily fee. You will flip at this house.

Migis Lodge, South Casco, on Sebago Lake, Maine 04077. Innkeepers: Gene and Grace Porta. Telephone: 207-655-4524. Six rooms in main inn, 25 cottages, all with private bath. Fireplaces all over. Open from late May to mid-October. Ninety acres with trails through the woods, on a sparkling lake. The names of the cottages give you a clue to what you will find, from Moonrise, Spruce and Driftwood, to Skylark. Accommodations are charming, with gay patchwork quilts used as spreads, ☞ fresh fruit in each room, and two great people, Gene and Grace, keeping everything all together. ☞ All boating, except for motor, is free to guests, and there is marvelous fishing. Water skiing is scheduled daily, and there are just loads of wonderful, relaxing things to do. Wednesday afternoon there is a cookout on an island. And you can play tennis on three clay courts.

The Moorings, Shore Road, Southwest Harbor, Maine 04679. Innkeepers: Betty and Leslie King. Telephone: 207-244-5523. Thirteen rooms, all with private bath. Open from late April through October. Continental breakfast, dinner, bar. Parking. Assorted prices. Take I-95 to Bangor, one hour on alternate Route 1, then turn left and go one mile on Route 102A. Or fly into Bangor or Bar Harbor. Children are welcome here in this most nautical Maine inn. All the rooms in the main house have names of Maine-built ships. There are picnic tables, bikes, canoes, and clamming equipment for house guests. Boat rentals and sailing lessons are available. The view of the harbor is sensational.

Newagen Inn, Newagen, Maine 04552. Innkeeper: Joseph Flood. Telephone: 207-633-5242. 70 rooms, with bath and telephone. Open mid-June to mid-September. Orchestra Saturday nights, bar, TV, fireplace. This lovely world away in time was founded in 1923 by Joshua Brooks, and his spirit still lingers. There is a sun-tempered saltwater pool, and beautiful, lovely silence. Four hundred acres of spruces, wooded trails and rocky, cove-studded shoreline surround the inn. There is a sweet lady who is described as an unobtrusive director of activities; I think this means she will help you find a fourth at bridge.

Rock Gardens Inn, Sebasco, Maine 04565. Innkeeper: Dot Winslow. Telephone: 207-389-1339. Four rooms in main inn, nine cottages, all with bath. Fireplaces in cottages. Breakfast, lunch, dinner, no bar, BYOB. Open mid-June to late September. Keep going beyond the Sebasco Lodge, and you will come to Rock Gardens Inn, on a rocky point sticking out into the Atlantic. Life is informal here, but if you like a lovely garden, come and stay awhile. The Winslows have been running the place for 35 years. There's one entree at night, but if you *can't* have lobster, there will be something else. It was pot roast the night I was here, especially for non-lobster eaters. It smelled delicious. In July and August reservations are for a minimum of one week, on a Saturday to Sunday basis. Advance arrangements are suggested.

Spruce Point Inn, Boothbay Harbor, Maine 04538. Innkeepers: John and Charlotte Druce. Telephone: 207-633-4152. 65 rooms with bath, 12 fireplaces. Open June 15 to September 15. Cottages. Write for rates. TV, two pools, three tennis courts, boating, moorings. You might call this a summer resort, but the country inn feel is here. Once you drive through the gates onto the peninsula that *is* Spruce Point, you are away from the workaday world. The Druces have been running things here for 17 years, and they know what they are up to. Sunday night there is a cruise around the harbor, with pastries and coffee. Monday morning try the cookout breakfast. You will find places for viewing the sunset and the rising moon. You must see the bar, the most unique boater's heaven that has ever crossed her bows.

The Squire Tarbox Inn, RFD #2, Box 318, Westport Island, Wiscasset, Maine 04578. Innkeepers: Elsie White and Anne McInvale. Telephone: 207-882-7693. Eight rooms, two with private bath. Fireplaces. Open May 1 to October 31. Dinner by reservation, liquor license. ☛ The food is sumptuous, prepared by Anne and offering two entrees each night. The original house was built in 1763, and in 1806 it was moved to its present location and bought by Squire Samuel Tarbox. The exposed boards and timbers that remain today are all original. In about 1825 the Squire built the main house. All has been well preserved. Wiscasset, the nearest town, is known as the prettiest town in Maine.

Whitehall Inn, Camden, Maine 04843. Innkeepers: Ed & Jean Dewing and family. Telephone: 207-236-3391. 38 rooms, 34 baths. Open June 1 through October. Breakfast, and dinner, lunch for house guests, bar. Parking. For 70 summers there have been guests at Whitehall Inn. The Dewings are new at innkeeping but believe in all the old traditions, from finger-bowls to beds that are turned down at night. Camden is a beautiful, interesting town. Poetess Edna St. Vincent Millay stood up in the parlor in this house and recited her long poem, "Renascence," to guests. Her high school diploma is framed on the wall, for here is where she was educated. There is a telescope for watching boats in the bay, and comfort unknown away from the busy highways.

And Just a Bit South of New England

The coast of New England is girded by famous, old Route 1, and it seemed a pity to ignore this grand highway when it leaves Connecticut and plunges into New York. If you follow it for its entire length you will find a sign that says, "Route 1, Mile 0". It is against a fence in Key West, Florida. Immediately to your right at the end of Duval Street is The *Pier House*.

This is old Key West where a sunset is a celebrated daily habit. A man with an iguana strolls by or you listen to a congo beat, or you watch incredible magic shows. It is all here at Mallory Square every day. Or you can enjoy the sunset at The Pier House, sipping a cool drink in their ☛ rooftop bar. It is very comfortable up here watching the rituals of the world's greatest sunsets.

The guest rooms and suites are sumptuous. The ☛ terraces afford you unmatched views, and the food ranges from the elegant gourmet cuisine of The Pier House restaurant to the conch fritters served in a paper basket at the outdoor bar. Their ☛ Key lime pie, I know from experience, is a thing of joy. None better. And oh those stone crabs!

I do believe you can tell I like it down here, not a country inn but a beautiful resort. Write or call for rates 1-800-327-8340. The Pier House is at One Duval Street. Air Florida jets you there from Miami in 35 minutes. I have driven down about 25 times. It is an interesting trip. Take your choice of car or plane but do go.

Index

Index

Other Globe Pequot Books
for your further travelling pleasure

Guidebooks:
A Guide to New England's Landscape
Factory Store Guide to All New England
Guide to Martha's Vineyard
Guide to Nantucket
Guide to New Bedford, Massachusetts
The Best of the Berkshires
Handbook for Beach Strollers
Historic Walks in Old Boston
Guide to the Ski Touring Centers of New England

Short Walk Books:
On Long Island
In Connecticut
On Cape Cod

Short Bike Ride Books:
In Connecticut
On Long Island
In Greater Boston and Central Massachusetts
On Cape Cod, Nantucket and the Vineyard
In the Berkshires
In Rhode Island

Available at your bookstore or direct from the publisher. For a free catalogue of New England books, write: The Globe Pequot Press, Old Chester Road, Chester, Connecticut 06412

About the author

The "inn creeper" is the nickname Elizabeth Squier has earned in her almost 10 years of researching this guide to the inns of New England. And a deserved name it is, for she tours more than 300 inns every year from top to bottom, inside out, before recommending the best ones to you.

A recognized authority on fine food and lodging, Elizabeth is a gourmet cook and has written travel and food columns for many periodicals. Like you, she recognizes readily the special ingredients that make a good inn exceptional.